FROM

STRESSED

TO

CENTERED

Rick,
I APPRECIATE OUR
YEARS OF learning one Another.
"STAY CENTERED" :)

Ordering Information: Special rates are available on quantity purchases by corporations, associations, and others. For details, please direct inquiries to www.fromstressedtocentered.com.

Produced by,
Sea Hill Press Inc.
P. O. Box 60301
Santa Barbara, California 93160
www.seahillpress.com

ISBN 978-0-9908354-0-0

Printed in the United States of America

FROM

STRESSED

TO

CENTERED

A Practical Guide to a Healthier and Happier You

By
Dana Gionta, Ph.D.
&
Dan Guerra, Psy.D.

DEDICATIONS

Dana's Dedication

To my parents, whose lives, values, and love taught me to embrace life.

To my clients, with whom I've had the extraordinary privilege of working with, learning from, and laughing with over the years.

Dan's Dedication

To my mother, who loved and laughed abundantly.

To all beings who have experienced suffering or have been impacted by someone else's suffering.

ACKNOWLEDGMENTS

This has truly been both a journey and an adventure for us. To our surprise, the writing and collaboration parts have been the easiest, and most natural. We are very grateful for this. To our readers: It is our hope that after reading our book, you feel that it is possible for you to move in the direction of a healthier, calmer, and happier life, one step at a time.

We would also like to thank all those who helped us bring this book to you. Their expertise, dedication, wisdom, and support were beacons on our journey.

Sea Hill Press for their continuity, consistency, availability, and know-how in the areas of editing, book designing, and navigating the trickier parts of the publishing world.

Danielle Mehta, our book landing page and Dana's website designer extraordinaire. You truly put your heart and passion into creating a highly informative and beautiful page for us, as well as a visually stunning website. You exceeded our expectations!

Miladinka (Meella) from 99 Designs, who beautifully crafted our book cover design and whose professionalism, dedication, and positive attitude are bar none!

A big thanks to Paul Marciano, Ph.D., for his advice and direction on how to publish our book.

To David Ballard, Jessica Peterson, and Janet Johnson, from the Center for Organizational Excellence of the American Psychological Association, for kindly providing us with the most up-to-date data from their "Stress in America" surveys.

And to Dawn Kamerling, owner of The Press House, for her enthusiasm to share our work and her public relations savvy.

To our friends, family, colleagues, and Facebook buddies, who took the time to pick their favorite book cover and book title. You made a part of putting this book together fun!

Dana's Personal Acknowledgments

With deep gratitude and joy, I have had the opportunity to work with many wonderful and courageous clients through the years. Many of the concepts, examples, and practical strategies in this book come from my work with you. Your positive feedback and enthusiasm regarding the message of our book made the challenging moments a little easier. I would like to thank Leslie for humorously coining the "B" word, which became the abbreviated word for boundaries, and is in our book!

A special thanks to be part of an amazing network of women through Savor the Success. The enthusiasm, support, laughter, business savvy, and resources of my Savor Circle women have helped make it a wonderful experience so far.

Additional thanks to Kristen Ballelli, David O'Brien and Tim Bray, who helped make the early part of this journey lighter with laughter, guidance and appreciation.

To my dear friends and loved ones over the years—Kathleen Giles & my lovely nieces, Isabella and Maya Grace; Sivanie Shiran, Beth Logue, John Costas, Jose Feliu, Daria & Greg Hong, and my magical nephew, Thomas—who have provided love, laughter, encouragement, support, and constructive feedback along the way. A special thanks to my sister, Daria Hong, for her editing finesse! Much love to you all!

Dan's Personal Acknowledgments

It is with a profound sense of gratitude and appreciation that I thank the following people for their expertise, encouragement, guidance, and support along the way: Dawn Kamerling, Joseph Guerra, Roseann Guerra, Alexander Rich, Ph.D., Kery Kilgannon, Conny Brunner, Karen Cianci, Ph.D., Della Dumlao, Cheryl Arrowood-Martens, Werner Schneiter, Anil Behal, Patrick Williams, Martin Singer, Jon Kabat-Zinn, Chris Bass, Helen Bass, Alastair Onglingswan, Leo Shea, Ph.D., and to every client and patient that I have been honored to work with.

CONTENTS

INTRODUCTION

With the advance of technology, economic challenges, and increasing demands on our time and energy, life can often feel overwhelming, hectic, and even unmanageable. Often, we find ourselves either in a chronic stressful environment or responding to our lives in stressful patterns that put our health and well-being at risk. Moreover, many of us have a general sense that something is wrong, but we may not really know what to do to change or improve it. This is understandable; however, this is not how anyone wants to feel over the long term.

How much can you relate to the following statements?

"Life has become too unmanageable."

"I have lost my ability to feel peace and joy in my life."

"I know something needs to be done to change my situation, but I just don't know what to do!"

"I have been trying to cope with my stress through behaviors that I know are unhealthy (smoking, drinking, overeating)."

"I am always either chronically worried or chronically stressed."

"Other people are always telling me that I need to care for myself better. I am not sure I even know what that means."

"I worry that my health won't hold up under this amount of stress."

Stress management and self-care create the foundation for good health and well-being. Our purpose for writing *From Stressed to Centered: A Practical Guide to a Healthier and Happier You* is to provide you with a clear understanding of how good self-care practices and stress management can improve your emotional and physical health and overall quality of life.

We recognize that intellectual understanding is not enough to help you make the necessary changes. In this book, we provide evidence-based strategies and practical tools to get your life back on track and help you feel more in control. We also have included vignettes throughout the chapters of this book to provide you with real life examples and applications of stress management and self-care. When you review these vignettes, please keep in mind the principles and practices for stress management and self-care offered in this book.

We would like this book to serve as a guide that you can take with you and refer to often, making it easier for you to apply new favorite tips and tools to improve your life. It has been our experience personally and professionally—and through extensive research review—that reaping the benefits of good stress management and self-care comes through both understanding and practice. Understanding happens by way of retention, and you retain much more by doing and doing repeatedly than you do by merely reading or hearing.

It does not matter where you begin or which steps you decide to take first; the most important point to remember is to take some sort of action, even if that action is initially a small one. The wonderful thing about change is that small changes become large ones over time. Steps in one area of your life often trickle over into other areas without any additional effort on your part. This will become clearer as you read through the chapters ahead.

It is our hope that this book will be used as both a springboard to your taking action and a guide you can take with you as you navigate your own journey toward stress management and self-care.

Enjoy the self-discovery along the way!

Our Personal Stories

Dana's Story

There are times in our lives that are demarcated by a specific event, like the birth of a child, getting a long awaited pet, or traveling abroad for the first time. Some describe these moments as life "before" and life "after," and others refer to them as "life-stopper events." I have had several such moments, some felt very positive, and others felt devastating at the time.

The first was the sudden, traumatic death of my father when I was in my mid-twenties. I didn't yet have the concept of self-care in mind. However, the seeds were planted by the strong recommendation of a kind and gifted grief therapist who told me to "be gentle with myself" during this time of recovery. I had never heard those words before.

Two years later, in 1997, my mother was diagnosed with a progressive health condition that we knew would eventually end her life. However, no one knew how long she had. I found myself running what best could be described as an emotional (and physical) marathon, with many unexpected detours on an emotional roller coaster. My sister and I began caring for her, which taxed every resource I had. It was, however, one of the most rewarding experiences of my life, for which I am forever grateful. At the time, the uncertainty of not knowing how long she had—perhaps one, three, or five years—was extraordinarily stressful. It was then that the concept of self-care sprouted. I realized that if I didn't begin to take better care of myself, I wouldn't survive this caregiving marathon.

I found myself running—my body decided this; my mind was on the couch ☺. I began swimming, taking naps in the afternoons, getting massages, taking weekends away, and more rarely, taking full weeks away—brief respites from caregiving. I sought the support of family, friends, and God to help me cope and accept the reality I knew was coming. A little over two years later, this period of my life ended.

In 2004, my self-care truly took root. Like many life-stopping events, mine happened very unexpectedly. This was the year I was diagnosed with cancer—a type I had never heard of before. It was then that I knew I had to make my self-care a priority—especially my emotional health. In addition to eating healthier and exercising to strengthen my immune system, I intuitively knew I had to make other life changes. I became very mindful of reducing my stress: avoiding any person or situation that was negative or draining, setting and holding to strict boundaries, assertively communicating my needs, and making fun and leisure time more of a priority. Fortunately, the type of treatment I chose and needed was mild, which I did for several years.

My body responded very well, and I had a very positive, consistent recovery. Many years later, after relocating, I was informed by a well-known specialist in this area that I had been misdiagnosed, that my condition was not cancer. Regardless of what the truth is, I have much gratitude, and a greater appreciation for my life.

My approach to self-care, especially my emotional well-being, was born through all of the above experiences, which I now integrate into my professional work—whether doing coaching, therapy, or workshops. Experiencing how beneficial it was (and is) in my own life, and witnessing how positive and empowering it has been for my clients over many years, I am able to say that I know this to be true. Self-care, both physical and emotional, does matter and will make an extraordinary difference in the quality of your life!

Dan's Story

I first became aware of the need for dealing with the stress in my life as a high school athlete. While I always excelled in most sports and enjoyed physical activity a great deal, I had the added attribute of someone who put a great deal of pressure on myself to perform well in many areas simultaneously. In many ways, the pressure I put on myself allowed me to work hard in sports with determination and grit. Hard work undoubtedly contributed to many of the successes that I had in sports and other areas of my life. However, the athletic pressure I put on myself—in combination with the pressures of maintaining good grades, being a very involved student, and having many responsibilities at home—may have inhibited me from performing at an optimal level. Who knew about stress management at age fifteen?

It wasn't until I matured as an athlete that I began to understand the very real connection between internal pressure of the mind and external performance of the body. This learning became all too clear during the grueling training we went through, specifically in the sport of wrestling. Wrestling is both an internally and externally demanding sport. Ask anyone who has wrestled competitively and, most likely, they will tell you that they never have trained harder for anything. The sport requires that you practice intensely for three to five hours per day, six days per week, often with little to no food (wrestlers typically train their weight down to one or two weight classes lower than their normal body weight). This meant sometimes losing twenty to thirty pounds off an already lean body (if only I were that lean now!). All that training would be challenging enough, yet I also faced the mental pressure of knowing that the person I was about to compete against across the wrestling mat also went through the same training process as me. Only half the battle was complete by the time I stepped on the mat.

We had a fantastic wrestling coach who always emphasized the importance of cultivating "intestinal fortitude" (guts) during our training. His approach and style trained us to develop an internal focus as one way to support and improve our physical performance during a wrestling match. This was compelling. Our mental state during training and before matches had an important influence on the outcome of those matches. It was no surprise, therefore, that practices were always geared toward mental training and visualizing positive outcomes—searching inside to gain the energy to push ourselves to run the three flights of stairs (sometimes with our partner of equal or more weight riding on our backs) for that one more minute, or giving that extra push in the seemingly endless round of wind sprints. It was easy to let negative thoughts, beliefs about oneself and one's opponents, concerns about upcoming matches, and the effects of outside pressures have a negative impact on performance.

As competitive sports took less of a central role in my life and new important life issues surfaced, I began to notice, understand, and value how the mind-body connection was having a significant benefit to areas beyond athletic performance. These included moods, states of well-being, concentration, expression of emotions, overall physical health, interpersonal relationships, and performance in academics.

As I entered doctoral graduate training in clinical psychology, it had become apparent that across the globe there was a great landscape of research and practice in the area of stress management that was capturing the attention of health-care practitioners and patients who suffered from stress-related illnesses. Coinciding with my graduate training was my personal study in the area of Eastern approaches to healing the mind and body from distress. The contemplative studies that caught my attention were mostly in the area of the deeper dimensions of yoga philosophy, yoga-inspired mind-body practices, and mindfulness meditation. Eastern approaches to mind-body health further solidified my belief that Western medicine alone had long neglected (or at least did not fully understand) the intimate connection between mind and body and the role it played in wellness and healing. My exposure to this broad and inspiring area of study sparked great interest in devoting much of my career to discovering bridges between Western medicine and psychology and Eastern approaches to mind-body healing. I had traveled through

India, Laos, Thailand, Indonesia, Australia, and New Zealand discovering many interesting and profound approaches to health and well-being.

My first real opportunity to practice bridging Eastern and Western approaches to mind-body healing came when I worked as a graduate assistant in The Stress and Habit Disorders Clinic under the tutelage of my mentor in psychology and behavioral medicine, Alexander Rich, PhD, a senior professor at Indiana University of Pennsylvania. I jumped at the chance to have the practical experience of working with patients who appeared in some ways to be so cut off from how their minds and bodies communicated that they suffered greatly from stress and the ravages of stress-related illnesses. In that clinic, we addressed and treated the psychological maladies that accompanied such medical problems as migraine headaches, tension headaches, Raynaud's disease, panic attacks, high blood pressure, and many forms of chronic pain. As psychologists, we also contributed to the direct modification of those disorders through modifying the psychological and emotional components of the illness in question. We used various methods of treatment, including biofeedback, diaphragmatic breathing, progressive muscle relaxation, hypnotherapy, and other evidence-based stress management techniques. It was very exciting to witness how patients soon benefited from just a little practice in the area of stress management, eventually came to have a healthy change in perspective on their health, and often experienced a positive change in their physical health and wellness.

The shift in perspective, one that is central to this book, is to understand that we have a responsibility to tune into our lives in such a way that raises our awareness of mind-body states so that we can proactively have an influence on our life experience when it comes to health and well-being. This process includes responding in healthy ways to our relationships both personally and professionally, ascribing meaning to our lives, and fulfilling our potential as human beings.

Having responsibility for our own health and wellness is not the same as blaming ourselves for unfortunate medical conditions or events that leave our health challenged. However, it is an invitation to become involved in our own health and wellness experience so that we realize that we are not powerless or helpless in the influence we can have on our health. Moreover, the influence that we do have does not have to be overbearing or burdensome. Oftentimes, the old adage of a little goes a long way has good application here.

Once awareness occurs that there is a relationship between stress and our well-being, it is no longer a huge leap to see how we can begin to positively impact our lives through effective stress management. Personally, I began to realize that the time I put into addressing my own stress levels through time-tested and evidence-based stress management techniques was well worth it and contributed to a more manageable and richer experience of life.

We hope you can identify with some pieces of our stories. We trust that in the chapters ahead you will begin to discover, develop, and celebrate your own personal stories as you start or continue your journey into good self-care and stress management.

Chapter 1

Introduction to Stress

Reality is the leading cause of stress amongst those in touch with it.

—Jane Wagner

The hardware store on the corner where I (Dan) sometimes make key copies has a sign of a fraught-looking cartoon character that is saying, "Let the Stress Begin!" In contrast, I have a friend who has a coffee mug that reads, "For Stress Relief, Resign as Manager of the Universe." You may find it interesting that the message from the hardware store sign gives us the impression that stress is an unavoidable, outside force that impinges upon us and leaves us frazzled. The second message, however, suggests that stress has more to do with our way of being, or a belief about ourselves that if reconsidered will lead to greater relief. Is one more accurate? It may be that both are important.

We can easily relate to aspects of stress that come from outside sources like morning traffic, work deadlines, or construction noise, as just a few examples. Perhaps more challenging is the idea that stress is also associated with internal sources such as our thoughts, perceptions, expectations and beliefs about our experiences, as the coffee mug example suggests.

How many of us can relate to the following internal thoughts and beliefs?:

"I must do this project perfectly."

"I am the only one who can handle this correctly."

"If I don't complete all the items on my list, then I am a failure."

"I am not being productive if I am resting."

Or on the more extreme side . . .

"I must have it all together at all times, otherwise my world will fall apart!"

Stress in Your Life

We have some work to do! The good news is that throughout the following sections, our aim is to help you understand and evaluate the stress in your life so you can make small, positive changes that can have a large and lasting impact!

Let's start with considering the following statements about stress. Which of the following statements do you most relate to? Rank them (1-10) in priority from most to least relevant in your life:

1. I am the type of person that gets stressed out easily. _____

2. If you had my kind of job, you would be stressed too! _____

3. There are outside forces that are causing stress in my life. _____

4. Stress seems to depend on the mood that I am in. _____

5. My thoughts keep me up at night. _____

6. Life handed me a bad hand. _____

7. I have to keep everything under control in my life; otherwise, nothing will get done. _____

8. Everything seems like it is just one step away from falling apart. _____

9. Stress will increase or decrease, depending on my reaction to it. _____

10. There are not enough hours in a day to keep my stress under control. _____

Internal or External Factors

Your ranking may tell you a little bit about your current beliefs and current approach to dealing with stress. It may also begin to help you identify whether your understanding of stress is based on internal or external factors. Items 2, 3, 6, 8, & 10 are primarily external associations to stress while 1, 4, 5, 7, & 9 are internal associations. Do you favor one over the other?

Consider bookmarking the page so you can revisit this section periodically to see how you are progressing, what insights you are gaining and possibly, how your rank order has changed.

As you read this book, consider holding both external and internal sources of stress in your mind, so that you may be open to understanding each more deeply. By doing this, you will be well underway to developing a healthy and effective approach to managing the stress in your life.

It may be helpful to define what we mean by this word "stress." Next, let us take a look at some definitions of stress.

What Exactly Is Stress?

"Stress" is a word that has multiple meanings depending on the context and emphasis. Let's consider the following definitions and examples:

> *Stress is a particular relationship between the person and the environment that is perceived by the person as either taxing or exceeding his or her resources and endangering his or her well-being.*

We may relate to this definition when stress is used in the following ways:

"I am so stressed out!"

"You are giving me stress!"

"Stress is getting the better of me."

"I am under a lot of stress."

We may also view stress more scientifically, as in the following definition:

> *Stress is "a physical, chemical, or emotional factor that causes bodily or mental tension and may be a factor in disease causation"* (Merriam-Webster's Dictionary).

Here, we may see stress used like this:

"The impact of stress on the nervous system . . . "

"He suffers from a stress-related illness . . . "

"Stress has an impact on the immune system."

Another definition of stress is "giving particular emphasis or importance to," and here, it refers to action as in the following:

"Let me stress how important this is."

"Stress the accent on the first syllable."

"Stress the importance that everyone be there on time."

Finally, we may have some familiarity with the word "stress" as it is used in the material world. Stress can be understood as the rate of wear and tear on an object as it adapts to change or outside influence.

"There is too much pressure, which is causing stress on that suspended beam."

"The weight of that object is causing significant stress."

"Excessive stress on the structure led to its collapse."

How Stress Shows Up

Now that you have familiarity with the definitions of stress, you may have begun thinking about how this applies to you personally. Most of us can all rattle off at least two or three ways stress shows up in our lives with hardly even thinking about it. Let's do just that.

Without thinking too much about it at this stage, write down a few examples of how stress is presently showing up in your life.

Before we go into a more detailed list of how stress presents itself, let us consider some research findings on stress. The remaining sections in this chapter display a comprehensive list of relevant statistics on stress and its relationship to illness, mental health, wellness, work, and other important areas of our lives. You can spend some time looking at the comprehensive list or you might choose to just focus on the parts of these sections that matter most to you. We find it to be compelling and fitting to the purpose of this book.

Some Stress Data

The American Psychological Association (APA) has done extensive survey research on attitudes and perceptions of stress dating back to 2007 as part of its campaign to promote mind/body health. The APA Stress in America™ survey data (2013) reveals a strong link between the mind and the body, and therefore, reveals significant implications about the connection between stress and physical and emotional health.

GIONTA & GUERRA
FIGURE 1. A STRESS SNAPSHOT.

American Psychological Association. "Stress In America 2013: Infographics" apa. org.http://www.apa.org/news/press/releases/stress/2013/infographics.aspx (Accessed December 12, 2013).

The following section, based on the most recent available data (2013), provides some interesting and relevant statistics on the impact of stress in various aspects of our lives (see Figure 1: A Stress Snapshot).

The Impact of Stress

Stress is so commonplace in American culture that a Google search generates millions of results with essays, opinions, and long descriptions on what stress is and what it is doing to us.

Since its inception, the Stress in America™ survey (American Psychological Association, 2013) has explored the place that stress has in American life and the impact it is having on our health and wellness. Survey findings illustrate a scenario in which Americans consistently experience stress at levels higher than what they think is healthy. And while the average level of stress may be declining, people have a hard time achieving personal stress management goals. Many people still report extreme stress (an 8, 9, or 10 on a 10-point scale), and even more say their stress has increased in the past year.

- On a scale of 1 to 10 (where 1 is "little or no stress" and 10 is "a great deal of stress"), adults report their stress level is 4.9 compared with 5.2 in 2011, 5.4 in 2010 and 2009, 5.9 in 2008, and 6.2 in 2007. Comparatively, Americans believe 3.6 is a healthy level of stress.

- Almost three-quarters (72 percent) of respondents say that their stress level has increased or stayed the same over the past five years, and 80 percent say their stress level has increased or stayed the same in the past year. Only 20 percent said their stress level has decreased in the past year.

- The number of Americans reporting extreme stress continues to be high. Twenty percent said their stress is an 8, 9, or 10 on a 10-point scale, which is comparable to the numbers reporting extreme stress in 2011 (22 percent), 2010 (24 percent), and 2009 (23 percent).

- Over the past five years, 60 percent of adults have tried to reduce their stress. More than half (53 percent) are still trying to meet this goal.

- Only 37 percent of Americans feel they are actually doing an excellent or very good job of managing their stress.

- Top sources of stress include money (69 percent), work (65 percent), the economy (61 percent), family responsibilities (57 percent), relationships (56 percent), family health problems (52 percent), and personal health concerns (51 percent).

- High and constant stress levels can negatively affect a person's physical and mental health. In addition to the ongoing mental strain, stress affects people physically; not everyone copes well.

- Americans continue to recognize the impact of stress—66 percent believe their stress has a moderate, strong, or very strong impact on their physical health, and 63 percent believe the same for their mental health.

- Approximately seven in 10 Americans report that they experience physical (69 percent) or non-physical symptoms (67 percent) of stress. Symptoms include irritability or anger (37 percent), fatigue (37 percent), feeling overwhelmed (35 percent), and changes in sleeping habits (30 percent).

- In addition, many people are not coping effectively with stress: People report lying awake (42 percent), overeating or eating unhealthy foods (36 percent), and skipping meals (27 percent) in the past month due to stress.

- Despite the negative effects stress appears to be having on people's physical and mental health, there is good news in terms of ways people cope with stress. More people appear to be making healthier stress management choices.

- More people are turning to exercise to manage their stress (52 percent compared with 47 percent in 2011).

- Sedentary behaviors like listening to music (48 percent), reading (40 percent), or watching television or movies for more than two hours per day (34 percent) continue to be popular strategies for managing stress.

- Unhealthy behaviors like eating and drinking alcohol to manage stress are on a steady decline. Twenty-five percent of Americans report eating to manage stress compared to 34 percent in 2008. Thirteen percent report drinking alcohol to manage their stress compared with 18 percent in 2008.

- More people appear to place importance on healthy behaviors this year. The survey found that more than half of people say it is extremely or very important to manage stress (64 percent in 2012 vs. 61 percent in 2011), eat healthy (60 percent in 2012 vs. 54 percent in 2011), or be physically active (57 percent in 2012 vs. 54 percent in 2011), yet they continue to have a hard time accomplishing these goals.

- Only 37 percent say they are actually doing an excellent or very good job at managing stress.

- Only 35 percent say they are actually doing an excellent or very good job at eating healthy.

- Only 33 percent say they are actually doing an excellent or very good job at being physically active.

Despite their interest in making changes for a healthier life, many adults face barriers that prevent them from achieving their health and wellness goals.

- For those who have been recommended to make a change or have decided to make a change, they say the following barriers prevent them from actually making lifestyle or behavior changes: lack of willpower (31 percent), lack of time (22 percent), the cost of making the change (16 percent), and stress (12 percent).

- While many adults acknowledge barriers to more effectively
  managing their stress and making healthier lifestyle
  and behavior choices, they appear to appreciate the role
  psychologists can play in mental and physical health care.

- More than half of adults think psychologists can help people
  a great deal or a lot in coping with mental health issues (56
  percent), and almost half (47 percent) think psychologists
  can help with stress management. Forty-two percent believe
  psychologists can help with making lifestyle or behavior
  changes, and 33 percent think psychologists can help them
  with issues of work/life balance. Despite their perceptions
  about the role of psychology in living healthier lives, only 6
  percent report that they see a mental health professional or a
  psychologist to help them manage their stress.

The Connection Between
Chronic Illness and Stress

- The Stress in America survey found that U.S. adults with a
  chronic illness seem to lack support for stress and behavior
  management when compared to Americans overall and
  compared to those who do not have a chronic illness.
  Americans with a chronic illness are less likely than those
  without a chronic illness to say they are doing enough to
  manage their stress (59 percent versus 66 percent). And for
  those with a chronic illness (who say they get little or no
  stress management or behavioral support from their health
  care provider), stress is on the rise; 41 percent said their
  stress increased in the past year compared with 35 percent of
  Americans overall.

- Although Americans living with a chronic illness see their
  health care provider more frequently than those without a
  chronic illness, people living with a chronic illness do not
  necessarily receive better stress management support. Half of
  those with a chronic illness (51 percent) see their health care
  provider three or more times annually compared with only

17 percent of those without. Despite more frequent visits, only one-quarter (25 percent) of those with a chronic illness say that they get "a great deal or a lot" of stress management support from their health care provider. But those who say that their health care provider supports them a great deal or a lot for stress or behavior management fare much better than those who do not receive such support. Sixty-eight percent of the former group report they are doing enough to manage stress. This compares with only 54 percent who say they receive little or no support.

These statistics speak for themselves. The results of these surveys show that stress is on our minds and has a significant impact on many areas of our lives.

Work-Related Stress

Let's take a look at how stress affects one area that for most adults, accounts for a very large chunk of how we spend our time: work.

The American Psychological Association's (APA) Center for Organizational Excellence has provided reliable information about stress in the workplace. Excerpts from their Psychologically Healthy Workplace Fact Sheet are listed below.

Work Stress

- Job stress is estimated to cost U.S. industry more than $300 billion a year in absenteeism, turnover, diminished productivity and medical, legal, and insurance costs (Rosch, 2001).

- More than one-third of American workers experience chronic work stress, with low salaries, lack of opportunity for advancement and heavy workloads topping the list of contributing factors (American Psychological Association, 2013b).

- Just 42 percent of employees say their organizations promote and support a healthy lifestyle, and only 36 percent report regularly participating in workplace health and wellness programs (American Psychological Association, 2013b).

- In 2001, the median number of days away from work as a result of anxiety, stress, and related disorders was twenty-five days; substantially greater than the median of six for all nonfatal injury and illness cases (Bureau of Labor Statistics, 2001).

Work-Life Balance & Flexibility

- Just over half of employees report that their supervisor supports their work-life balance (57 percent) and that their organization values work-life balance (55 percent; American Psychological Association, 2013a).

- Only 39 percent of American workers report that their employers provide options for flexible work, and 30 percent say their employers provide benefits that help them more easily meet their non-work demands (American Psychological Association, 2013b).

- One-third of working Americans (33 percent) say that work interfering during personal or family time has a significant impact on their level of work stress, and one in four report that job demands interfere with their ability to fulfill family or home responsibilities (American Psychological Association, 2013b).

- "Sandwiched" employees, defined as those who are responsible for child care and the care of parents, are at a greater risk for depression (Neal & Hammer, 2007, p. 208).

- Work-family conflict is related to general psychological distress and self-reported poor physical health (Frone, Russell, & Barnes, 1996).

Work-Related Communication Technology

- Despite the clear advantages that technology brings to the workplace, 36 percent of employees report that rather than lighten their workload, communication technology increases the quantity of work. Additionally, almost a quarter of working Americans (23 percent) say that communication technology forces them to work faster (American Psychological Association, 2013a).

- Today's "always on" culture makes it more difficult to disconnect from work, with more than a third of working Americans reporting that communication technology makes it more difficult for them to stop thinking about work (34 percent) and to take a break from work (35 percent); (American Psychological Association, 2013a).

After considering all that data on stress and thinking a bit about your own life, let's pose a question: How do you know when you are personally experiencing unhealthy levels of stress? Put another way, when does simple stress become prolonged and unmanageable, transforming into *distress*? Understanding the period of time and space in your life where stress transforms to distress is very much the crux of the stress management portion of this book and will help you to zone in on how to manage stress better in your life. Finding out when and how stress transforms into distress in your life may be more difficult to assess than you first think, due the complexity of the stress experience.

One approach emphasizes increasing awareness of your personal stress signs and symptoms as an important first step. Without good awareness, stress remains present yet outside of your sphere of influence. A good place to start is getting to know your own signals of stress. Let's take a look at the physical, emotional, cognitive, and behavioral signals of stress in the next chapter.

Chapter 2

Stress Indicators

Our awareness of how stress operates in our lives can start with looking toward indicators or signs where stress shows up. These signs tend to manifest in our bodies, through our feelings, in our minds in the form of thoughts, and eventually in the way we act and behave in the world with others.

The following is a list of stress indicators. Make some notes or check marks next to the indicators that may apply to you.

Physical Indicators of Stress

Rapid heart rate without physical exertion

Chronic headaches

Difficulty falling asleep or staying asleep

High blood pressure

Significant weight loss or gain

Neck and lower backaches

Chest pain

Digestive issues such as indigestion, vomiting, diarrhea, and/or constipation

Increased frequency of urination

Dryness of the throat and mouth

Increased susceptibility to illness, including increasing frequency of colds and flu-like symptoms

Reduced sexual appetite (reduced libido)

Feeling nauseous or dizzy

Feeling exhausted or drained

Premenstrual tension

"Butterflies"

Excessive perspiration

Emotional or Feeling Indicators of Stress

Apathy

A feeling of being "on edge"

Irritable mood

Irritability or quicker to anger

Chronic worry

Anxiety

Fear of failure

Feeling overwhelmed

Depressed (chronically sad) mood

Feelings of unworthiness

Feeling "keyed up" or "on edge"

Feelings of loneliness or isolation

Cognitive or Thinking Indicators of Stress

Trouble concentrating

Forgetfulness

Negative thinking or dwelling on negative thoughts

Racing thoughts

Poor judgment

Easily embarrassed

Preoccupation with thoughts or activities

Thoughts of suicide

Behavioral Indicators of Stress

Difficulty making decisions

Difficulty organizing or keeping track of things in our lives

A change in eating habits

Sleeping more than usual or difficulty getting to sleep

Quicker response to emotions like anger and sadness

Using alcohol or drugs (including cigarettes) to relieve, distract, or forget about our stress

Teeth grinding (including when asleep)

Use of drugs to relax (including cigarettes, alcohol, and illicit drugs)

Nervous habits (i.e., nail biting, being easily startled, stuttering, nervous ticks, trembling)

Isolating yourself from others

Procrastinating or neglecting responsibilities

Not all of the symptoms above are caused by stress exclusively. It is important to note that some of the indicators above may be symptomatic of medical or psychological conditions other than stress. In the case of a medical or psychological condition caused by factors outside of stress alone, further investigation by a qualified, licensed medical or mental health professional is recommended. If you are experiencing one or more of the indicators above, you should strongly consider consulting a licensed medical or mental health professional for further clarification of symptoms.

Now that you likely have some familiarity with your personal stress indicators, consider what might be some of the causes of stress in your life. In other words, what situations or scenarios may lead to prolonged levels of simple stress, thereby leaving your vulnerable to experiencing distress?

Chapter 3

The Holmes-Rahe Social Adjustment Scale

Happiness comes from . . . some curious adjustment to life.

—Hugh Walpole

Holmes and Rahe (1967) helped assign a number value to stress based on an individual's perceptions of life events. Their work gave credence to the notions that

(1) all life events involving change, even positive change, result in some level of stress, and

(2) stress associated with life events are subject to perception.

The Holmes-Rahe Social Adjustment Scale was based on a study of 394 individuals who were asked to assign values to various life events after being told that marriage was assigned a value of 50.

There is no score to obtain on this scale. Instead, it can be used as a guide to show the relative impact of stressful events on a fairly large number of individuals. The numbers on this scale do not signify actual values of stress, and you may rate a particular event as higher or lower based on your own experience.

Take a look at this list to see what life events may contribute to stress in your life now. You may also choose to add your own events (and values) to the list if you believe significant ones are missing.

EVENTS	SCALE OF IMPACT
Death of Spouse	100
Divorce	75
Marital Separation	65
Prison Term	63
Death of Close Family Member	63
Personal Injury or Illness	53
Marriage	50
Dismissal From Work	47
Marital Reconciliation	45
Retirement	45
Change in Health of Family Member	44
Pregnancy	40
Difficulty in Sexual Functioning	39
Gaining a New Family Member	39
Business Readjustment	39
Change in Financial State	38
Death of Close Friend	37
Change to a Different Line of Work	36
Change in Number of Arguments with Spouse	36
Large Mortgage or Loan	31
Foreclosure of Mortgage or Loan	30

Change in Responsibilities at Work	29
Son or Daughter Leaving Home	29
Conflict with In-Laws	28
Outstanding Personal Achievement	26
Partner Begins or Stops Work	26
Beginning or Ending School	25
Change in Living Conditions	24
Revision of Personal Habits	23
Conflict with Boss	20
Change in Work Hours or Working Conditions	19
Change in Recreation	18
Change in Social Activities	17
Small Mortgage or Loan	16
Change in Sleeping Habits	16
Change in Eating Habits	16
Change in Number of Family Get-Togethers	15
Vacations	13
Holidays	12
Minor Violations of the Law	11

Causes of Stress in Your Life

Consider the major causes of stress that have been most present for you in the last year. Write down the top five causes of stress in your life in the space below. Feel free to choose causes of stress from the list above in the Holmes-Rahe Social Adjustment Scale or from causes that you came up with on your own.

The top five causes of your stress in the past year:

1. _____

2. _____

3. _____

4. _____

5. _____

Chapter 4

Guerra-Gionta
Stress Inventory

*Future shock [is] the shattering stress and disorientation
that we induce in individuals by subjecting them
to too much change in too short a time.*

—Alvin Toffler

The Guerra-Gionta Stress Inventory was developed by researching fairly common, everyday life circumstances that have some relationship to stress. The purpose of this inventory is to raise awareness of how stress shows up for you personally. It will also help to provide you with a connection between the scale of The Holmes-Rahe Social Adjustment Scale and your own personal stress experience.

Taking the Guerra-Gionta Stress Inventory

Please read the following statements and circle the number that best describes how well each statement applies to you.

Use the following key:

1 = not at all
2 = somewhat
3 = neutral
4 = mostly applies
5 = directly applies to me

I have moved residences in the last year.

1   2   3   4   5

I have gone through a divorce or separation in the last five years.

1   2   3   4   5

I am dissatisfied with my job.

1   2   3   4   5

I have had trouble falling asleep or staying asleep in the past two weeks.

1   2   3   4   5

I have a mortgage on my home that requires monthly payments.

1   2   3   4   5

I got married within the last year.

1   2   3   4   5

I have changed jobs or am expecting to change jobs in the next year.

1   2   3   4   5

I am having marriage problems.

1   2   3   4   5

I lost my job in the last two years.

1   2   3   4   5

I am living with a chronic medical condition.

1   2   3   4   5

I am the primary caregiver for someone with a chronic medical condition.

| 1 | 2 | 3 | 4 | 5 |

I am retired from my work or thinking about retiring from my work.

| 1 | 2 | 3 | 4 | 5 |

I have significant financial debt.

| 1 | 2 | 3 | 4 | 5 |

I am living with one or more teenagers at home.

| 1 | 2 | 3 | 4 | 5 |

More times than not, I feel overwhelmed at my place of employment

| 1 | 2 | 3 | 4 | 5 |

I feel close to someone with a significant drug and/or alcohol problem.

| 1 | 2 | 3 | 4 | 5 |

My son or daughter has left home or is planning to leave home in the next year.

| 1 | 2 | 3 | 4 | 5 |

I play or watch competitive sports regularly.

| 1 | 2 | 3 | 4 | 5 |

I believe that I have more things to do than time allows for.

| 1 | 2 | 3 | 4 | 5 |

I believe that I have little to no control over the quality of my life.

1   2   3   4   5

I have few people in my life who give me support.

1   2   3   4   5

My life is controlled by outside circumstances.

1   2   3   4   5

I am planning to take a vacation in the next three months.

1   2   3   4   5

I have been spending a lot of time with family members lately.

1   2   3   4   5

I have experienced the death of a loved one in the past three years.

1   2   3   4   5

Scoring the Guerra-Gionta Stress Inventory

Use the following scoring key:

25-48   = low stress
49-74   = medium stress
75-100 = moderately high stress
101-125 = high stress

Now you have hopefully begun to create a map of how stress shows up in your life. Of course, within that map there are many hills and valleys, borders and open areas, winding roads, open highways, and some dead ends. We recognize that there are nuances and varied expressions of our own personal stress responses and that the map is not always straightforward or decipherable. Not to worry! We suggest that you look at understanding your own stress experience as a dynamic and changing process, and one that will be better understood and managed in time.

Reviewing Stress Experiences

After reviewing the data based on research by Holmes and Rahe and after taking the Guerra-Gionta Stress Inventory yourself, you may notice that negative experiences are not the only contributors to stress. Positive events such as moving into a beautiful, new home, getting married, or starting an exciting career can have strong effects on the nervous system and, therefore, have a strong impact on your experience of stress.

So far, we have learned that stress not only derives from external sources such as highway traffic or a heavy workload at the office, but also can come from internal sources such as how we perceive, experience, and react to a given event or person. We have also now learned that a great deal of stress can be the result of negative experiences such as the loss of a loved one or unemployment; however, stress can equally be derived from positive events such as getting married, being promoted or playing for a local sports team who just made it to the playoffs!

Keep in mind the fact that not all stress is bad. Did you know that stress is also necessary for our survival? We will begin to look at the nuances of stress, learn when it is adaptive, and also learn under what circumstances it is maladaptive in the next chapter.

Evaluating Stress

Before we move on, as a way to reinforce our learning so far, take a look at the photos in Figure 2: Evaluating Stress. Which of these images remind you of stress?

From the images that remind you of stress, first decide whether the stress derives from an external or internal source of stress. Next, think about whether or not the stress is positive, negative, or maybe even both.

FIGURE 2. EVALUATING STRESS.

Make some notes on your impressions of the images in Figure 2, keeping in mind external or internal sources and whether the stress is positive, negative, or both:

_____

_____

_____

_____

_____

_____

_____

_____

Chapter 5

Surviving, Striving, and Thriving with Stress

Pain is a relatively objective, physical phenomenon; suffering is our psychological resistance to what happens. Events may create physical pain but they do not in themselves create suffering. Resistance creates suffering.

—Dan Milman

Before we make the mistake of wishing that our stress were gone forever, we want to develop a more sophisticated and useful understanding of stress and its function. The truth is that we need stress to survive, strive, and thrive! Athletes count on stress to perform optimally. Students thrive (and sometimes take a "dive" in grades) from stress when taking tests and giving presentations. All of us rely on stress responses to know how to quickly and effectively address a potentially threatening situation.

Let's take a look at this graphically in Figure 3: Yerkes-Dodson Law:

FIGURE 3. YERKES-DODSON LAW.

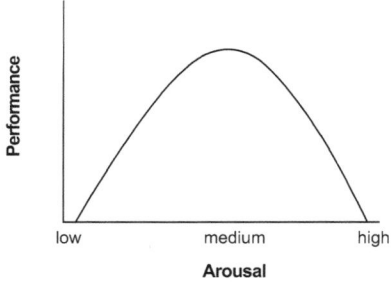

Priest, S. (1990). The Adventure Experience Paradigm. In J.C. Miles, & S. Priest (Eds.), Adventure Recreation, (pp.157-162). State College PA: Venture Publishing.

As we look at the graph above, you see that arousal (one measure of stress) and performance have an interesting relationship. The relationship between arousal and performance appears to be curvilinear, which basically shows that as arousal increases from low to medium, performance also increases. It also shows that as arousal increases from medium to high, performance decreases. We can conclude that a medium amount of stress is necessary to perform well. These findings are the result of research from two psychologists from the early 1900s named Yerkes and Dodson, who scientifically discovered and made known the curvilinear relationship between arousal and performance. It is important to note that different tasks require different levels of arousal for optimal performance. For example, a complex intellectual task may require lower levels of arousal to facilitate focus and concentration, whereas a task demanding stamina, such as long distance running, may be better achieved through higher levels of arousal, which would improve motivation.

In summary, we all need a certain level of stress to perform well in whatever we do. For most of us, problems come when our arousal and resulting stress is at a high level for an extended period of time. Under this circumstance, the level and duration of arousal may not match the task we are performing and often impairs our performance on the task or tasks we are undertaking.

The next section deals with what happens in the nervous system with regard to stress. Those of you who become stressed out at the mere mention of biological or neurological terms may want to skip this section and go straight into action in Chapter 7.

In either case, it is important to mention that we all have a fight-or-flight response and a rest-and-digest response embedded in our nervous system that operates to speed up or slow down the stress response in our body and mind. This chemical-electrical mechanism is much like the accelerator and brake of a motor vehicle, which responds to external and internal situations that arise and call for either speeding up or slowing down.

Chapter 6

Neurophysiology of Stress

*What lies behind us and what lies before us are tiny
matters compared to what lies within us.*

—Henry Stanley Haskins

Walter B. Cannon, a Harvard physiologist whose work was published around the turn of the twentieth century, gave us the notion of the fight or flight response, which described how the nervous system, organs, and physiological systems deal with perceived or real threats to our safety. In primitive times of human life, when humans were living in more basic and often harsher conditions, there was a real need for effective ways to respond to daily dangers. Fighting or fleeing from (flight) larger mammals, or even competition for survival against other tribes and peoples, were common parts of life. Walter B. Cannon's research discovered that humans were actually hard wired for this adaptive response through the nervous system. Contrasting the fight-or-flight response is the rest-and-digest response, which takes place at times when perceived or real danger is absent, a response that also appears to be hard wired for adaptation.

You may remember from high school biology class that the human nervous system is comprised of a central nervous system and a peripheral nervous system. An important part of the peripheral nervous system, and the focus of our discussion here, is the autonomic nervous system, or ANS. A basic understanding of the ANS will give you a better understanding of the relationship between stress and your physiology. Since the purpose of this section is only for a cursory understanding of these concepts, take heart, we are aware that these terms may be new to you (or may even trigger stressful memories in some). Our hope is to explain these concepts in digestible ways. We believe a basic understanding of stress and physiology can be useful in managing stress better.

The ANS is divided into two branches: (1) the sympathetic nervous system and (2) the parasympathetic nervous system. These two branches function largely below the level of consciousness and both affect heart rate, digestion, respiration rate, salivation, perspiration, pupil diameter, urination, and sexual arousal. Some actions of the ANS work more in tandem with the conscious mind, such as breathing.

Sympathetic and parasympathetic branches of the ANS appear to function mostly in opposition to each other. However, they are more aptly complementary than antagonistic (working against each other). You may conceive of sympathetic branch as the accelerator (fight or flight) and the parasympathetic branch as the brake (rest and digest). The sympathetic branch of the ANS is typically involved with actions related to arousal and energy and sometimes inhibition, as with digestion. The parasympathetic branch is typically associated with resting and calming actions and also promotes digestion.

The functions of the autonomic nervous system can be seen in Figure 4: Autonomic Nervous System. Let's take a look at some of their respective actions more closely.

Sympathetic Nervous System

Diverts blood flow away from the gastro-intestinal (GI) tract and skin through a process called vasoconstriction.

Enhances blood flow to skeletal muscles and the lungs.

Dilates the bronchioles in the lung, which allows for greater oxygen exchange.

Increases heart rate and the contracting action of cardiac cells called myocytes (this allows for the enhanced blood flow to skeletal muscles).

Dilates pupils, allowing more light to enter the eye and enhances far-sighted vision.

Vasodilation occurs in coronary vessels of the heart.

Constriction of intestinal and urinary sphincters.

Inhibits peristalsis.

Stimulates orgasm.

Parasympathetic Nervous System

Dilates the blood vessels leading to the GI tract, increasing blood flow. As there are greater metabolic demands placed on the body by the gut during food consumption, this process enhances digestion.

Sometimes constricts the diameter of bronchioles in the lung when the need for oxygen has diminished.

Dedicated cardiac branches of the vagus and thoracic spinal accessory nerves impart parasympathetic control of the heart or myocardium.

Constricts the pupils, allowing for enhanced nearer-sighted vision.

Stimulates the salivary gland, increasing salivary secretion.

Accelerates peristalsis mediating digestion of food and, indirectly, the absorption of nutrients.

Involved in the erection of genitals.

Stimulates sexual arousal.

Today, life does not often come up against the types of threats that concerned us in harsher times such as attacks by wild animals or the need to find appropriate shelter for the night. The fight or flight response, however, is still quite relevant in current times. Modern life presents a myriad of its own form of threats, such as technology demands, enabling

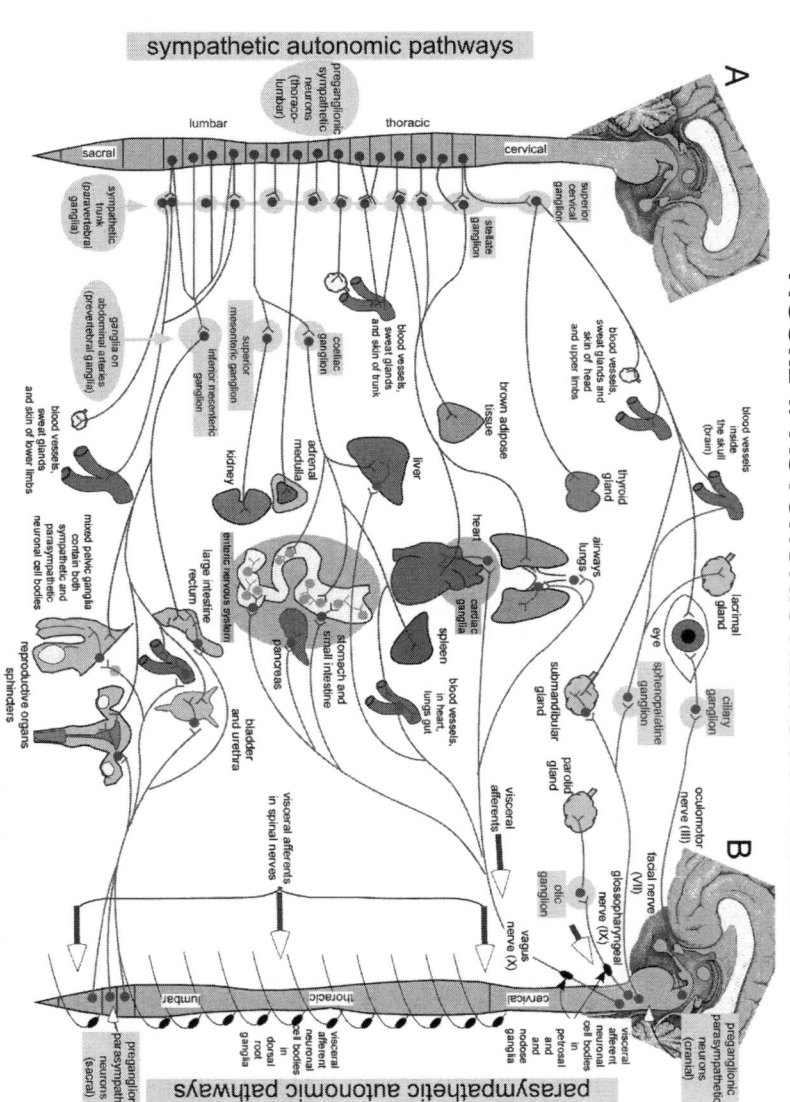

FIGURE 4. AUTONOMIC NERVOUS SYSTEM.

Blessing, Bill & Gibbins, Ian. Scholarpedia.org http://www.scholarpedia.org/article/Autonomic_nervous_system (Accessed January 15, 2014).

and requiring us to do more in shorter amounts of time: multi-tasking, seemingly impossible deadlines, often unattainable work demands, and mounting frustrations. This, coupled with economic crises in recent years, certainly influences our nervous system.

Whenever we find ourselves responding to real or perceived threats over long periods of time, we have sympathetic nervous system (fight or flight) over-responding. In a simpler vernacular, for many individuals stress can become so commonplace that chronic flight or flight has become a way of life rather than an adaptive response to an occasional threatening situation. This is something to be taken seriously since we run the risk of some psychological, emotional, or physiological impairment with prolonged sympathetic nervous system over-responding. In small doses, stress is not all that bad. In fact, as we have seen earlier, stress can even help us perform under pressure and motivate us to do our best. In contrast, when we are constantly responding in an emergency mode, our minds and bodies can pay a price.

Chapter 7

Three Components of Stress Management

Smile, breathe and go slowly.

—Thích Nhât HAnh

It can be encouraging to know that the practice of stress management is very simple. Simple does not always mean easy when it comes to learning a new skill or finding motivation to practice; however, there may be some relief at least in knowing that the mechanics of managing stress are not complicated at all. Successfully managing your stress basically boils down to gaining awareness, understanding, and skill in three fundamental areas:

1. The breath

2. The body

3. Our thoughts

The Breath

Breathing is a just about the most fundamental aspect of human existence. It is the first thing we do when we enter this life and the last thing we do when we leave it. The breath is made up of a cycle that is composed of four essential parts: (1) an inhalation, as we take breath in; (2) the pause between the inhalation and the exhalation; (3) an exhalation, as we expel our breath out; (4) the pause between the exhalation and the inhalation. This vital cycle is responsible for so many things including bringing oxygen to our cells and ridding the body of many toxins through expelling carbon dioxide.

If breathing marks the beginning and end of our life, sustaining and upholding us throughout the lifespan, then we cannot ignore its significance. However, many people are scarcely aware of their own breath. This becomes evident when we learn to observe our own breath or even while observing others breathing. Many of us do not really breathe as functionally and as effectively as is possible. The breath is often interrupted, shortened, held, and constricted by a variety of factors in life.

Cigarette smoking and exposure to environmental toxins are just two of examples of outside influences on the breath. However, the breath is also impacted by our inner world—the world of thoughts and emotions.

Learning to Breathe

Our thoughts, feelings, imagination, and even our muscle tension affect the way we breathe. This is important because the implication is that if we learn to become more aware of, and skillful with, our inner life, we will have greater influence over it; subsequently, we will have a greater positive influence on the way we breathe.

You will learn more by doing than by seeing or hearing. Learning comes from putting this knowledge into practice. In Chapter 9, you will be introduced to a practice that will help you learn to become more aware of, and skillful with, the breath.

DEALING WITH THE UNEXPECTED

Denise was leaving her apartment to meet a colleague of hers in the city. There was a lot to plan before she left. They were planning on writing the last chapters of their book. She needed all her materials: papers, flash drives, reference books, and printouts—not to mention her bathing suit, hiking boots, and water bottle since they were heading up to the country to have a couple of days of work and play. It looked like she had everything and was going to make it on time, but as she opened her door to leave the apartment, a bird flew right into her home!

When she arrived in New York City, a place where one almost needs special training to survive driving, she could not find a parking spot. Her colleague said he would be on the NE corner of 42nd and Lexington, but with all the people standing around, she couldn't find him. Not to mention that just last week she got a $115 ticket for waiting in the car for a friend for no longer than five minutes!

STRESS MANAGEMENT STRATEGIES

How should she deal with this?

Denise could employ breath observation practice to begin to calm the nervous system and prevent a full-blown move into the fight-or-flight mode.

If Denise is already in the fight-or-flight mode, breath observation could help alleviate tensions so she can return to a rest-and-digest mode.

Denise could also become aware of any negative thoughts about her situation and work toward replacing those negative thoughts with healthier, more affirming ones.

The Body

Our physical bodies, as wonderful and complex as they are, can be great registers of stress. This process has adaptive and maladaptive components to it, but suffice it to say that having some awareness and understanding of the body and how it is prone to registering stress can be very useful. It only takes a minimum amount of awareness to notice that when we are worrying, caught by surprise, fearful, or anticipating a negative event (or sometimes even a positive event); the body responds. The response that the body has to stress manifests in a myriad of ways. This could take the form of heart palpitations, sweating, a noisy or queasy stomach, or muscle tension, to name a few. Living in the Northeast, USA, I (Dan) often see individuals on the street braving the cold winter months by lifting their shoulders to their ears and tensing their muscles during the very cold days. This is one simple observation of how even weather can be a stressor that leads to bodily changes. Awareness of how the body changes during periods of stress is a good first step toward mastering stress management. We will have a look at a practice that has been scientifically proven to decrease stress through raising awareness and understanding of tension and relaxation in the body in Chapter 9.

Our Thoughts

Thinking is a tricky process. Most of us would agree quite readily that thinking helps us survive and even thrive in daily life. It is not a radical idea that thoughts are necessary, and in fact are a very useful part of our human condition. When we begin to think about how the process of thinking and thoughts influence stress, it usually does not take long to see how one influences the other. I would like to establish early in this chapter that thinking and its resulting thoughts are here to stay—and that, of course, is important. However, I would also like to invite the reader to consider that we have a relationship to our thoughts. This relationship basically can be understood as one between the thinker and the thoughts. That is, we are the thinker having thoughts. Our relationship to thinking creates a type of emphasis or value judgment that goes on almost imperceptibly. This can contribute to a great deal of stress, and prolonged stress leads to suffering.

Nature of Mind

We have to establish some concepts around the nature of mind. I don't mean this in some esoteric, metaphysical sense (although those levels might be interesting to consider at another time). I am addressing just the mechanics of mind that we often take for granted. The mind, one might argue, is a thought-producing machine. If we watch it for a moment—observe it or take notice of it—we quickly see that it is active, tenacious, constantly moving, and not prone to giving up easily. Often it takes very provocative events, or at least a somewhat forcible shift in our experience, to help quell the mind of these active qualities, even for a minute. For instance, if you are like me, most of the day the mind is occupied with basically two temporal (time) dimensions:

> The first is the past: what happened; what went on; what he said; what she said; what he did; what she did; what I did; what I said; regrets; reflection; opinions.

> The second is the future: what will happen; what do I need to do; a list of things that must get done; worry; anticipation; predictions; risk assessment.

When the mind is firmly planted in the past or the future, it typically takes a rather striking event to shift it out of that mode. Striking or provocative events can help to shift the mind out of its past or future orientation:

> I bump into someone I really like or dislike on the street.

> I discover that I have crossed the street before the light turned green and a bus is hurtling toward me.

> A sharp pain in my body grabs my attention.

> I am playing a sport well and intensely.

> I am experiencing a significantly pleasurable moment.

> I am all involved in a crucial experience where every movement must be accurate for success or safety (rock climbing or climbing a very high ladder are good examples).

These are only a few examples of events that can shift the mind out of the usual mode of past or future orientation. These events stick us squarely in the present moment. Of course, it does not take long following these events for the mind to start getting pulled back to the past or future and to start creating a barrage of past- and future-oriented thoughts once again. Without developing a purposeful attention to this process, the risk is that we are often pulled to and fro by the mind and swept up in the movement of thought, an experience that can often result in discouragement, stress, worry, and anxiety. In a way, many of us walk through life battling with the mind, resulting in a great deal of consternation and suffering.

THE BENEFITS OF STRESS MANAGEMENT

Managing stress effectively has the following benefits (Shaar & Britton, 2011):

Physical: Better immune system functioning, reduced blood pressure, better digestive functioning, less muscle tension

Mental: Clearer thinking, better decision-making, easier ability to focus, better access to creativity

Emotional: Calmer, more centered, energized, and more positive mood states

Spiritual: Greater sense of meaning and purpose for your life

You Are Not the Mind

A novel concept to most Westerners is the idea that we do not have to live our lives in a way that identifies us too strongly with the version of mind described above. If we can begin to see that thoughts are really discrete events that are rising and falling in the mind (much like a car passing on the road is a discrete event, or an elevator going up and down all day with or without passengers comprises a series of discrete events), then we do not have to ascribe as much importance or cultivate what I call such "dangerous curiosity" about those mind events.

This dangerous curiosity is evident when we get involved in our thinking and thoughts in the same way we might get involved in a very dramatic and addictive soap opera. In the soap opera, we all know the characters, we can often predict what will happen next if we really think about it, and a part of us knows the topics and events are not always that meaningful or even believable. Despite this, our relationship to this drama is one that displays supreme interest, urgency, and belief. It is as if we were sitting at the edge of the chair yelling at the television trying to warn the character, "Don't go into that room!" or "He's lying to you; don't believe him!" We may be so engaged in this process that we lose attention and focus on what is going on around us. How many of us have had this hypnotic type of relationship with TV shows or movies at one time or another?

When managing stress it is important to shift out of this type of relationship to our mind to one that observes what is going on, without necessarily getting involved. Gurani Anjali, one of my first teachers, often referred to this type of healthy approach to mind as learning to be, "One hundred percent attached and one hundred percent detached."

Of course, there are exceptions to the suggestion for us not to get involved with our thinking. Balancing a checkbook, providing a rational argument when writing a philosophy paper, trying to give someone directions, and solving a mathematics problem are all examples of employing the mind and all of its thinking capacities in very useful and important ways. Relating to our thoughts in an engaged, focused, and enthusiastic way during these moments is useful and necessary. On the other hand, we can perhaps begin to cultivate other times when we are purposefully not getting involved with our thinking. This state can be viewed as one of relaxed attentiveness and one that watches thinking without being invested in the content of thinking.

You do not equal your thoughts.

It is common, and initially very difficult to see, that we are not our thoughts. After all, if we are intellectual creatures who place such high value on reason, logic, and developing solutions in the mind, it is almost heretical to suggest a process that might de-emphasize the importance of thought. But the fact is that most of our thoughts are unnecessarily aligned with anxiety (or depression) producing a valence (a charge) or meaning, which over time can lead to a great deal of stress.

So if we are not the mind, then who are we? Well, defining who we are in total is a very compelling and interesting question, but it is also beyond the scope of this book. What can be said for now is that if we can agree that who we are is something more than just mind and what mind does, then we may be able to begin practicing a new relationship with our mind that could alleviate stress. Before we move onto breath, body, and thought practices for stress management, let us first consider some important points in Chapter 8.

PRACTICE SECTION

Chapter 8

Beginning a
Stress Management Practice:
Goals and Expectations

A superior [person] is modest in speech, but exceeds in actions.

—Confucius

Starting something new in any area can sometimes feel daunting and overwhelming. When beginning a stress management practice, we believe it is helpful to think about how to make this new learning be as smooth and effective as possible. In the following section let us consider setting some goals around your stress management practice and discussing the importance of managing expectations (Davis, M., Eshelman, E. L. & McKay, M., 2008).

Goals

What are your goals? This is important because not everyone's stress management goals will be the same. One person may wish to try to systematically remove some of the outside stressors in his or her life. Another individual may want to learn one or two relaxation techniques that would result in lower blood pressure, thereby helping to potentially control hypertension. Other goals may be focused on developing awareness around how stress is impacting your life, how much stress is present, and where in your life it shows up the most (i.e., work, home, relationships). Another useful aspect to consider is whether stress tends to arise in the mind, body, emotions, or some combination of all three (Davis, M., et. al., 2008).

When creating your stress management goals, it is helpful to start with the end in mind. That is, you might ask, "What would my life or 'my world' look or feel like if I were able to have success in managing stress?"

Think about some of your personal goals for managing stress. Consider listing them below.

My goals for managing stress:

_____

_____

_____

_____

Expectations

There is no doubt that unmanaged stress over extended periods can sometimes lead to adverse physical consequences. However, this does not mean that all medical problems are caused by stress. Please have a physical examination by a licensed physician if you are experiencing maladies such as chronic headaches, chronic pain of any kind, high blood pressure, stomach problems, and heart palpitations. Let your physician know that you are planning to start a stress management practice, and ask your physician if there are any counter-indications to doing so.

The techniques and tools that you will find in Chapter 9 are not to be viewed as a panacea or magic bullet to solving problems. With that said, the techniques are very effective and have proven to be helpful to countless people suffering from the negative effects of stress. We recommend being extraordinarily patient with yourself and allowing yourself plenty of time to learn how to cope better with stress.

Starting with realistic expectations will better ensure success. Try writing down what is in your control and what is not in your control in your life. For instance, factors like your age, family members' attitudes and behavior, and perhaps your current financial situation may be not be in your direct control; whereas, how many responsibilities you take on in the next year, the way you think and appraise situations, and your behavior with regard to sleep, nutrition, and exercise may be possible to change with some effort.

Take a moment to write down in Figure 5 some life factors that you believe are in and out of your control with regard to managing stress.

FIGURE 5. FACTORS IN/OUT OF MY CONTROL TO MANAGE STRESS.

Factors that are out of my control to manage stress?	Factors that are in my control to manage stress?

Remember, not every stress management technique is suited for each person. And it is not necessary for you to become an expert in every technique in order to successfully combat negative stress. Instead, feel free to let yourself experiment with a variety of practices. Tune into which tool or technique that you feel most connected with and attempt to apply it.

Chapter 9

Practicing Stress Management

The greatest weapon against stress is our ability to choose one thought over another.

—William James

In Chapter 7, we discussed the importance of developing awareness, understanding and skill in three fundamental areas, in order to manage stress well: the breath, the body, and our thoughts. In this chapter, we will outline some stress management practices for each of these three fundamental areas.

The Breath Practices

Let's start with an easy practice of breath control.

Practice #1 — Breath: Breath Observation Practice

1. Get into a comfortable, upright seated position.

2. Let your seat be firmly planted evenly into the chair and imagine your torso is gently lifting out from your pelvis area so that the body is long and straight.

3. Allow your chin be parallel to the floor.

4. If you are comfortable, allow your eyes to close. If closing your eyes is not comfortable, stare at a small spot anywhere on the floor in front of you and keep your eyes focused there.

5. Without too much effort, allow yourself to become aware of your body and the sensation of your body as it makes contact with the chair and floor.

6. Specifically, take notice of the contact points between your back and the chair, your buttocks and the chair, your hands in your lap, and your feet touching the floor.

7. Now slowly and gently allow yourself to become aware of the fact that you are breathing.

8. Do not try to manipulate the breath in any way; just notice it. The most important part of this practice is to be committed to simply noticing the breath, not judging the breath, criticizing yourself, or making internal comments to yourself about the practice.

9. Give yourself some time to get accustomed to this form of paying attention. There is no need to rush; take your time.

10. After you practice this for some moments, you may notice the mind starting to wander. If the mind begins to wander, just remind yourself, without judgment or criticism, that you are practicing breath awareness, and bring yourself back to the practice.

11. Repeat this process within the practice itself.

Practice #2 — Breath:
*Ratio Breathing Practice: 4:4:8 Breathing**

You can use ratio breathing as a way to calm a very overactive and worried mind. It may also help you cultivate a state of mind that is sometimes called "relaxed attentiveness."

1. Get into a comfortable, upright, seated position.

2. Let your seat be firmly planted evenly into the chair and imagine your torso is gently lifting out from your pelvis area so that the body is long and straight.

3. Allow your chin to be parallel to the floor.

4. If you are comfortable, allow your eyes to close. If you are not comfortable closing your eyes, stare at a small spot anywhere on the floor in front of you and keep your eyes focused there.

5. Without too much effort, allow yourself to become aware of your body and the sensation of your body as it makes contact with the chair and floor.

6. Let your breath be comfortable and without strain. Simply notice your breath coming into the body and notice your breath leaving the body. Do this for thirty seconds or so.

7. In the next few moments you are invited to count your breath as it enters the body on the inhale. Count your breath in a way so that the length of your inhalation moves along to a count of four. Usually, one count per second (if you are able) works well.

8. When you reach the end (or the top) of your inhalation, you should reach the number four in your counting.

9. Now, hold the inhaled breath for a count of two. In other words, hold the breath while you count, "one, two . . ."

10. Now, release the breath slowly in a loosely, controlled way, while counting to a count of eight.

11. When you reach the end of your exhaled breath, you should arrive at the number eight in your count.

12. Feel free to speed up or slow down your counting to a level that is comfortable for you.

13. You can pause for a moment or two before your next inhalation if you would like to.

14. Repeat steps 1-13.

*This practice can be carried out as instructed in a 4:2:8 ratio or can be adjusted to a 2:1:4 ratio, depending on the practitioner's abilities and development.

The Body Practice

Let us begin an easy-to-learn practice that helps the body release muscle tension and stress.

Practice — Body:
Progressive Muscle Relaxation (PMR) Practice

Progressive Muscle Relaxation (PMR) is a technique that takes us on a journey through the body and many of its respective muscle groups. The first point of focus is on the breath, and the next point of focus is on the body part or muscle group. In addition to focusing, we tense and release the muscles on or near that body part in order to become very skilled at knowing the difference between tension and relaxation.

With this practice, you will be on your way to relaxing the whole body and mind.

Caution

This is a tensing and releasing exercise; however, if you are having pain in any area of the body, please do NOT tense that area. Instead, when the instructions tell you to tense the area you should skip the tensing of that muscle group and just focus on the release.

Practice Tips

The practice takes you through the tensing and releasing of various muscle groups one time; however, for maximum benefit, it is good to repeat all tensing and releasing of body parts three times in sequence. This means that each muscle group is done three times in a row before moving on to the next muscle group.

Also, the time period between tensing and releasing depends on a few factors such as comfort level, ability to hold the breath, and level of familiarity with the practice. Feel free to adjust the time period and practice with different amounts of time. You may want to try letting three to five seconds pass in the "tensing" position as a start.

If you find this practice helpful, you may consider making a recording of your own voice taking you through the practice. This can be done on a smart phone or from your computer microphone.

The PMR Practice

Sit in a comfortable chair or lie down on a firm surface like the floor or a thin yoga mat. Do not lie in bed for this practice.

Become aware of your natural breath. Do not try to manipulate your breathing in any special way.

Just observe your natural breath.

Become aware of your hands. Take a deep inhalation and clench your hands into fists as you inhale.

Hold the breath for a moment or two.

Now slowly exhale the breath and release your hands totally. Feel the difference between tension and relaxation.

Bring your attention to your wrists.

Inhale the breath, and with your hands flat and open, bend your hands at the wrist joint so that your fingertips point up toward the ceiling, creating some tension in your forearms.

Hold the breath for a moment or two. Notice the tension.

Now release as you exhale the breath and just relax the hands completely.

Bring your attention to the biceps muscles.

Take an inhaled breath now and bring your fingertips up to the front of your shoulders and tense your biceps muscles here.

Hold the breath and notice the tension there. Study it.

Now slowly exhale and release the arms back down in full release. Time your release with the exhale so that you are letting go of the tension as you let go of your breath. Feel the difference between tension and relaxation. Feel calm, comfortable relaxation spreading now down the arms and into the hands.

Now become aware of your shoulders.

Take a deep inhalation, and lift your shoulders up toward your ears. Make sure to keep the rest of the body relaxed while you do this. Lift them and hold the breath. Sense the breath on hold and the tension in the shoulders. Now slowly exhale the breath and release the shoulders.

Very good.

Bring your attention to the back of your head.

Inhale the breath and gently push the back of the head against the floor, chair, or wall just enough to create some tension in the head and neck. Hold the breath for a moment or two. Study the tension there. Now release as you exhale the breath and bring the head back to normal position, relaxed and not touching anything.

Now bring your attention to your eyebrows.

First just sense the space above your eyebrows. Notice it.

Now take an inhaled breath and raise your eyebrows up . . . creating ripples in the forehead. See the tensions. Notice it. Hold it.

Now exhale and let the eyebrows fall down to normal position. Feel the relaxation spreading all along the forehead.

Now bring your attention to the eyes.

Inhale deeply . . . and as you inhale squeeze the eyes shut so that no light can get in. Squeeze them as you inhale and hold the breath. Notice the tension. With a conscious decision, release the breath now and let the eyes relax into a normal closed position now. Very good.

Take a moment to notice the relaxation in the head and upper part of the face.

And bring your attention now to the nose.

Inhale and scrunch the nose up, creating tension in the nose. You can imagine trying to bring all parts of the face to the center of your nose. Hold the tension there. Study it.

And exhale and release the tension in the nose. Feel the face flatten out. Enjoy the relaxation in your face.

Bring your attention to the teeth.

Very gently, allow the teeth to clench, not too hard, but enough to feel some tension in the jaw. Inhale and clench the teeth. Hold it and notice the tension.

Exhale and separate the teeth. Now wiggle the jaw a bit from left to right. Feel the release. We hold a lot of tension in the jaw, so it is nice to release this tension here.

Now bring your attention to the lips.

Inhale and press the lips together. Hold the tension there. Press them together. Notice the tension in and around the mouth.

Exhale and gently separate the lips on the exhale. Notice the release and relaxation all around the mouth now. Good.

Calm comfortable relaxation is spreading now through the whole head and face.

Let's bring the attention down to the neck now.

On an inhale, jut the chin forward a bit and bring tension in the neck by flexing the neck muscles. So many muscles in the neck. Feel them . . . feel the tension and study it. Keep the rest of your body relaxed as you tense the neck. Tensing one part of the body while relaxing the rest of the body is called differential relaxation. Hold the tension there.

Okay, now exhale . . . and with the exhale, release the tension in your neck. You are in control of the tension and the relaxation. With your breath you are able to let go. Tell yourself this. Good.

Focus your attention on the muscles in and around the chest.

Inhale and flex the chest muscles as best you can. Feel it. Again, keep your arms relaxed and head and neck relaxed. Feel the tension in your chest. Hold it!

Now release the tension as you exhale. Feel the release.

Bring your attention to the belly.

Inhale and tighten the belly a bit, almost as if someone were going to give you a little punch in the belly. Hold the tension there . . . brace for it. Notice the tension.

And now exhale and release the tension in the belly. Just let it go, and don't hold on to it at all. Many of us hold tension in the belly all the time. Let it go. Feel the difference between tension and relaxation.

Now shift your attention to the lower back.

Inhale . . . and very carefully, flex the lower back muscles arching the lower back just enough to feel a little tension there as you curve the spine. Notice that.

Okay now exhale and release the lower back. You can even release enough by rounding the lower back and dipping the tailbone down into your seat. Exhale and let go. Feel the release. Very good.

Bring your attention to your buttocks. Inhale . . . and as you inhale, tense the buttocks muscles right there in your seat. Feel it. Notice it. Study it. Hold the tension there. Now exhale and release the tension in the buttocks. As you exhale, feel the tension melting into your seat. Let it go completely with the exhale. Feel the difference between tension and relaxation.

Bring your attention to your thigh muscles. With your feet flat on the floor, inhale and tense the thighs by drawing the kneecap up toward your hips. Flex the thighs and hold the tension right there. Notice the tension.

Okay now exhale and release the thigh muscles. Feel the release and the letting go.

Now bring your attention to the calf muscles.

Inhale and raise the heels off the ground, creating tension in the calf muscles. Notice this tension here. Feel it. Study it and hold.

Now exhale and release the tension in the calves. Feel the release now. Feel the relaxation spreading through the whole of the legs.

And now bring your attention to your feet.

Inhale and scrunch up the feet into balls inside the shoes. The feet can hold a lot of tension, so just feel it here. Scrunch them up and hold the tension and your inhaled breath. Notice the tension.

Exhale now and release the tension by letting your feet spill out like water into your shoes again. Feel them widen and spread out as you release your breath. Very, very good! Sense the release.

Okay now, get ready for a full body scan.

We are going to focus on the whole body at once.

Inhale slowly and deeply . . . and as you do, tense the hands into fists, bring them up to the shoulders. Lift the shoulders, raise the eyebrows, press the lips together, tense the neck and chest, belly, and buttocks, tense the legs and feet. And hold, hold it all. Feel the tension and hold the breath.

Now with an audible exhale, release the tension and release the body fully. Let the tension of the body sink into the chair on the release and keep exhaling all the breath out of the body. Very good.

Feel all the comfort and relaxation that you have created all throughout the body.

Thoughts Practice

Working with our thoughts and thinking itself can be challenging, but this is a very worthwhile process when developing an effective stress management practice. Two practices are useful in working with thoughts. One is called "thought-stopping/thought-replacement" and the other is called "mindfulness" or "mindfulness meditation."

Practice #1 — Thoughts: Thought-Stopping and Thought-Replacement Practice

We do not have to be slaves to our thinking. Many of us go through the day with intense and worried thoughts that we believe we have no control over. If we can first identify thoughts that are producing worry or panic in the mind then we can practice a technique that has been shown to decrease stress throughout the day by halting the movement and augmentation of worried thoughts.

The first part of practicing this technique requires the practitioner to simply give the mind the command to stop when he or she is experiencing repetitive, worrisome, negative, or catastrophic thoughts. The second part of the practice is to replace that negative thought with something more positive and realistic.

The practice of thought-stopping with thought-replacement is effective because it provides an interruption of unhealthy thoughts through a stop command that serves as a reminder and a distraction. This practice, when used over time, also serves to raise awareness of unhealthy thought patterns, giving practitioners a greater sense of control and efficacy over their thought life, and therefore, their stress levels. Let's take a look in Figure 6: Thought Stopping Chart at how thought-stopping/thought-replacement works on a practical level.

FIGURE 6. THOUGHT STOPPING CHART.

1) Negative/Unhealthy Thought	2) Command	3) Positive/Realistic Thought Replacement
"I will never get all this work done!"	STOP!	"I will make a plan to get most of the work done by Friday."
"My life is falling apart."	NOT NOW!!	"I have big challenges that I will address one by one."
"Everyone will think that I don't know what I am doing."	STOP!	"I will not predict what others think, and instead, will consider and address each person one by one."
"Everyone is against me."	NOT TRUE!!	"Person X or Person Y is not treating me well right now for these (Z) reasons."

Charting Your Progress

Make a chart for yourself using the model above and list the negative/unhealthy thoughts that are most common to your experience and the ones that you suspect are giving you the most trouble with regard to stress. Fill in the positive/realistic thought replacement section. Make an intention to practice this method. Schedule dates and times through the day when you will practice this. It could go something like this:

> "I will practice thought-stopping/thought-replacement at the end of every work meeting."

> "I will practice thought-stopping/thought-replacement three times per day."

> "I will practice thought-stopping/thought-replacement at 10:00 a.m., 1:00 p.m., 4:00 p.m., and before I go to sleep at night."

Make a plan. Be consistent. Don't get discouraged. Like everything that is mentioned in this book, these practices take time to master!

Use the blank chart, Figure 7: Blank Thought Stopping Chart, to practice writing down some of the negative/unhealthy thoughts, a command, and a positive/realistic thought replacement that are specific and most related to you and your life.

FIGURE 7. BLANK THOUGHT STOPPING CHART.

1) Negative/Unhealthy Thought	2) Command	3) Positive/Realistic Thought Replacement

WORRIED MIND

I am Lara, and I am a seventeen-year-old high school senior. My parents were divorced when I was five years old. I am pretty popular and usually get good reports from my teachers. I play volleyball, which is cool, and I am looking for some scholarships to colleges this year. People are always saying that I have a lot going for me, but I feel like I am a total mess. I seem to always worry. I am worried about boys and worried about the way I look. I worry about getting into college, and then if I do get into college, I know I'm going to worry about paying for it. I had this one college interview, but I worried so much about it that when it was time for the interview, I couldn't even go because I felt too sick. My friends try to tell me to just chill out, but it doesn't seem to work. It's like everything that I am planning to do I think is going to end in some big disaster. It really bugs me. I know I'm talented, at least that is what others say, but I wish someone could just turn off the switch in my mind. At night I stay up late thinking about all these things, and I'm unable to make my mind shut up! Others seem to be able to relax with friends and family, but I can't ever sit still long enough to be able to feel relaxed. Am I just messed up?

STRESS-MANAGEMENT STRATEGIES

Worry is often the result of an overactive mind with an abundance of negative, and catastrophic thoughts. Thought-stopping and thought-replacement would help Lara.

Lara would benefit from a regular practice of mindfulness to begin experiencing a different orientation and perspective on thoughts and her worried mind.

Practice #2 — Thoughts: Mindfulness

Mindfulness has become quite the buzzword in the past decade or so. There is mindfulness meditation, Mindfulness Based Stress Reduction (MBSR) (Kabat-Zinn, 1994), mindfulness yoga, Mindfulness-Based Cognitive Therapy (MBCT), and the list goes on. In contrast to providing in-depth understanding of all the various facets and practices related to mindfulness, my intention here is to simplify the concept for the reader and to provide a very basic, introductory practice of mindfulness to help with managing stress. I (Dan) have included mindfulness in the "Thoughts" section of this chapter because I believe that mindfulness practice is very much connected to our relationship to mind and to our thinking.

In the section in Chapter 7 entitled "Nature of Mind," I alluded to the concept that it is the very essence of mind to continue to churn out thoughts all day. In a way, it is the mind's primary purpose! There are some meditation practitioners who focus on stopping the mind from thinking too much and others who focus on words or phrases (mantras) that are repeated over and over again as a point of focus for the mind that is something other than "thought" in its usual form. The way that I introduce mindfulness and mindfulness-as-meditation is to introduce the concept that *we are aware* and that awareness is our make-up. Additionally, each of us has a different level of awareness at any given time. Psychotherapists sometimes look at this as conscious mind, subconscious mind, and unconscious mind in their grossest forms. If we can entertain this mind-as-awareness concept as true for the moment, then it may also be true that we can train the mind to become more aware of *what is* through willingness, observation, and attention. The benefits of harnessing one's attention and awareness are numerous. Somehow, if we are able to tap into awareness in a fuller form, there appears to immediately be a shift in our life experience in those moments.

Here are some reports on the physical and psychological benefits of practicing mindfulness:

Calmness of mood

Decreased anxiety

Better control over chronic pain

Being able to experience what is happening now (versus the mind getting stuck in the past or future)

Decreased symptoms and better management of some autoimmune disorders

Increased creative problem solving

Less impulsive and quick to "fly off the handle"

Better ability to manage stress levels

More self-management of emotions

Mindfulness Practice

Sit in a comfortable, straight-back chair. Your feet are touching the ground. Place your hands in your lap.

Your head and neck are relaxed and even along the shoulder's axis. Allow your chin to be parallel to the floor and adopt a posture that is upright, dignified, and erect—not slouched over yet not militaristic either.

If you are comfortable with it, allow your eyes to close. If not, you can leave them open a little as you stare at a spot on the floor about twelve inches or so in front of your feet.

In the next moments, become aware that you are breathing. Become aware of your full inhalation, as the breath comes into the body, and your full exhalation, as the breath leaves the body. Refrain from manipulating the breath or changing it in any way. Instead, just tune into the breath.

This tuning into the breath is a never-ending cycle . . . And paying attention to your breath this way may tend to change your perception of time . . . Continue to tune into the breath, and feel the sensation of the breath as it moves up the body . . . through the belly and past the sternum, then out toward the rib cage and up through the chest, filling the collarbones and continuing all up the neck and head and into the nose. And as you exhale, feel the same cycle again. Feel the breath as it moves down the throat, into the neck and collarbones, down past the chest, into the sternum and ribs and ending up in the belly.

Now, if it makes sense, you can begin to breathe in a way so that on the inhale, the breath moves down deep into the belly and the belly expands on your inhalation. And as you exhale, the belly falls back down toward the spine. Some of you may get this right away, while for others, it may seem counter-intuitive. If this belly breath does not come to you after a few breaths, just forget it for now, and you can go back to observing the flow of the breath, just as it is.

Continue this observation of breath . . . from moment to moment.

You may find, from time to time, that the mind can get busy. Thoughts may come up, and those thoughts may be about all kinds of things.

Use this opportunity, when thoughts arise in the mind to see that as a signal to gently bring your attention back to the breath. Do this in a gentle way, not harsh or judgmental toward yourself. Thoughts keep coming, but you don't have to get involved with them. Just let the thoughts rise and fall within your awareness.

As many times as the thoughts come is equal to as many times as you can bring your attention back to the breath.

The breath becomes an anchor for your attention . . . anchoring your sense of awareness and just tuning in right now to what is . . . not what happened in the past or what will happen in the future . . . but just getting interested and curious about the here and now. This present moment . . . and this one . . . And this one . . .

If you are new to mindfulness, continue this practice for five to ten more minutes. Remember to use your breath as a point of focus . . . become interested, for this time period, in the breath. Use the breath as an anchor to bring you back to the present moment.

In the last few moments of this practice, recommit to being right here now with the breath.

And now, as you finish the practice, take a moment to forget about awareness of the breath. Bring your awareness to your body sitting in the chair . . . the whole body.

Tune into it for a moment . . . sense the light in the room coming through your eyelids . . . and then slowly open your eyes . . .

This mindfulness practice is finished.

Where, When, and How Often to Practice These Techniques

Where?

One method is to find a place that is soothing, quiet, and uninterrupted during your time of practice. Another line of thinking says that there is no perfect time or place to practice stress management, so be courageous and willing to bring the practice to wherever you are, despite the conditions. In either case, finding a place and time to practice does not have to be fancy or elaborate, but you may find these suggestions helpful:

> A clean, comfortable, small space in one of the rooms of your apartment or house
>
> An accessible, uninterrupted part of your office or office building like a seminar room or break room
>
> Time outdoors in nature like a beach or lake, the woods, on top of a mountain, or even in the park
>
> On the subway or public transportation (be sure that your belongings are secured, however)
>
> In your parked car (remember most of these tools should not be used while driving)
>
> Believe it or not, even in the middle of a conversation with a spouse, partner, boss, or child is a good time to practice some aspects of stress management.

A few words on finding a place where you will not be interrupted: Since practicing these techniques may be new to you, try explaining to others that you will be practicing techniques that help you to relax and manage stress. We find that most of your friends and family members whom you inform about your practice will be supportive and may even become interested in knowing more about what you learn! Think about where you could practice your stress management techniques and consider listing them below.

Top three places I would like to practice stress management:

1. _____

2. _____

3. _____

When and How Often?

The short answer to when you should practice stress management techniques is whenever possible, however, personally, I (Dan) find coordinating practice at sunrise, noontime, and/or sunset to be some of the most satisfying times to practice. How often you should practice is based on a number of factors including what is practical given your responsibilities and schedule, your level of motivation, and the time it takes for your learning of these techniques to develop. The following is only a guideline for you to consider as you develop your practice. Feel free to modify this guideline to fit your own needs and preferences.

> *Breath Observation:* As you begin this practice, try "formally" practicing two times per week at sunrise for two to five minutes each time. Work up to three times per week for ten to fifteen minutes each session. You can also begin practicing "informally" which means learning to observe your breath in your everyday activities and in between "formal" sessions, wherever and whenever you can.

> *Ratio Breathing:* As you begin this practice, try this practice two times per week at sunrise or anytime in the morning for five minutes each session. As it becomes easier, work up to ten to fifteen minutes per session.

PMR: This is a nice practice to do at sunset or ninety minutes before bedtime. Beginners may choose only the major parts of the body to focus on and spend ten to twelve minutes in the practice, one time per week, initially. As you progress, add more specific muscle groups and work up to twenty to thirty minutes, three times per week.

Thought-Stopping/Thought-Replacement: You can begin practice thought stopping formally, by setting up a time and place where you can record in a journal, frequent, negative thoughts that you wish to replace. As you write them down, you can also record replacement thoughts and refer to this journal daily. Once, you become familiar with your own thoughts and their respective replacements, you can engage in this practice throughout your day. If you have trouble remembering to do this, try setting up a time period (for example, each day somewhere between ten o'clock in the morning and twelve o'clock noon) where you will purposely practice this technique.

Mindfulness: This practice may be one that continues to develop and change across the lifespan. In the beginning, try practicing three times per week for two to five minutes each session. As you progress, work up to three times per week ten to fifteen minutes per session and eventually, daily anywhere from twenty to sixty minutes each session.

KEEPING CONTROL

Joe is a fifty-eight-year-old male partnered with Randi, his girlfriend, for over fifteen years. He has a great sense of humor, and Randi describes Joe as a control freak. Joe reports that he is happy in his relationship with Randi and does admit that he likes to be in control of things. Randi says that Joe becomes noticeably irritable and even nervous in situations where he no longer in charge of the situation. She humorously describes the set of events that took place once when they were traveling together:

> It was like traveling with a benevolent dictator! It wasn't enough that he had to choose the hotel, the whole itinerary when we were there, and where we ate dinner each night. He also made us arrive at the airport three hours before our departure time because he never trusts that there will be enough time to get to the airport on time or make it through airport security. This puts tremendous pressure on me and us to have everything "just so." Otherwise tension builds, and I can tell he is uncomfortable.

Joe only seems to feel comfortable when he believes that he has access to all the control buttons of his world in each moment. He does not use emotional language to discuss his stress as he looks rather surprised when others tell him he gets nervous or irritable. Joe does report difficulties with digestion and high blood pressure. His doctor recently suggested that he consider blood pressure medication to address his hypertension. Joe exercises, and Randi reported that this helps his mood in the short term, but exercise does not appear to have an impact on the overall picture of his stress.

SELF-CARE STRATEGIES

Joe can make use of a combination of ratio-breathing and progressive muscle relaxation to address his stress level and high blood pressure.

Joe would benefit from a regular practice of mindfulness meditation with a trained instructor. This practice will allow him to understand the movements and working of his thinking mind better and to learn tools to become more effective at handling situations in his outer life.

Joe may eventually learn that he, ironically, can gain more of the control that he wants by learning how to let go.

Chapter 10

Succeeding in Stress Management

Success is to be measured not so much by the position that one has reached in life as by the obstacles which he has overcome.

—Booker T. Washington

In order to have a successful and effective stress management practice, it is worth discussing obstacles, attitudes, and belief systems. Preparing yourself ahead of time for obstacles to good stress management will prevent you from getting caught off guard when beginning your practice. Your attitude can make or break your experience when attempting to manage your stress. And belief systems, thought to often emerge from attitudes, can have powerful effects on how successful you feel and how successful you are with respect to stress management.

Obstacles

An obstacle is anything that blocks your way or prevents or hinders your progress. Let's take a look at potential obstacles:

- *Time:* You need to carve out only a little time, regularly, to have a successful experience.

- *Impatience:* This may be a new practice to you. You may need to adjust your "patience barometer" to allow yourself some struggle and some significant time for growth.

- *Self-Sabotage:* This can take the form of cutting corners, talking yourself out of the need for the practice, or returning to old thought and behavior patterns that increase your stress level.

- *Interruptions:* Consider making a commitment to minimize disruptions, shut off smartphones, turn off email notifications, and make others aware that you need to be undisturbed for a period of time while you practice stress management techniques. If others respect you, they will honor this time. As your self-respect increases, you will facilitate this respect from others.

- *Lack of Perseverance:* Just like an athlete or good parent, do not give up, especially when you are presented with struggles, challenges, or perceived failures. One might adopt the idea that there are no failures, just opportunities for learning, growth, and change.

Personal obstacles in my life:

1. _____

2. _____

3. _____

4. _____

5. _____

Attitudes

An attitude is a disposition or a position with regard to a person, thing, tendency, or orientation, especially of the mind. Having a positive attitude is not the same as cheerleading yourself, adopting a Pollyanna attitude, or being in denial about what faces you. Positive attitude is about purposely adopting an orientation of mind that believes it will succeed as opposed to focusing or overvaluing the parts that don't seem to work. Let's take a look at some attitudes that promote healthy stress management.

- This is a great challenge. I am ready to face the challenge of managing my stress better. I look forward to the positive outcomes and the benefits that I will enjoy as a result!

- This is a fail-safe practice. As long as I am putting forth effort to practice and have the intention of improvement, I will view everything I do around this practice as progress, improvement, and a mini-success!

- I am a promoter of my own well-being and health. I am empowered and encouraged to participate actively in my own well-being and health. I have the skills and resources to do so and to do so effectively!

Consider thinking of other statements that, when practiced, would constitute the kind of positive attitude that would help you in your stress management practice. Make the statements personal and ones that you can relate to easily, or you can borrow one of the above statements in the meantime.

Personal positive attitude statements:

1. _____

2. _____

3. _____

4. _____

5. _____

Beliefs

A belief is a strongly held opinion or conviction that is spoken or unspoken. It is a psychological state in which an individual confidently holds that a proposition or a premise is true. We all are likely familiar with belief as a concept and may be aware of some of our own strongly held beliefs.

What we may be less aware of is that statements we make to ourselves, almost subconsciously, when repeated enough times transform into beliefs, and we may not even be fully aware that those beliefs are being created. These beliefs then have a strong impact on our motivation, behavior, and decision-making process. Let us look at some beliefs that would be in opposition to a successful and effective stress management practice:

- "I am unable to manage my stress."

- "I don't have the kind of personality that can let go."

- "I just cannot relax."

- "Other people seem to know how to relax better than me."

- "I should be doing something more than I am doing."

- "I cannot stop my thoughts."

- "Stress management is for people who are not busy."

- "If I slow down, I will no longer be as productive."

If you have the above beliefs, it will be very difficult to be successful in managing your stress. You will likely feel discouraged, unmotivated, and helpless if you focus on or emphasize these beliefs. Instead, you can consciously choose to change these beliefs into healthier, more effective viewpoints as a way to maximize the effectiveness of our practice.

Can you think of other beliefs that may get in the way of a healthy stress management practice? If so, write them down here. Even better, try to identify the ones with which you personally tend to struggle.

Personal beliefs I struggle with:

1. _____

2. _____

3. _____

4. _____

5. _____

Here are some effective thoughts that can transform into healthy beliefs, with practice:

- If I am willing to sit, breathe, and watch, then I am already practicing stress management.

- Don't just do something, sit there!

- Five minutes of stress management practice each day is significantly better than zero minutes of stress management practice each day.

- I may not be able to keep my mind on my breath 100 percent of the time, but each time I choose to purposefully pay attention to my breath, I feel better.

- I am able to learn, and I am learning how to be a better observer of my body and mind.

- I can both slow down and be productive.

- Managing my stress will help me manage my time more effectively and efficiently.

- The best leaders take time for reflection.

Consider thinking of other statements that when practiced would become the kind of healthy beliefs that would help you in your stress management practice. Make the statements personal and ones that you can relate to easily, or you can borrow some of the statements above in the meantime.

Personal beliefs I would like to adopt:

1. _____

2. _____

3. _____

4. _____

5. _____

You now have some tools, and hopefully you now have a solid awareness and understanding about how stress may operate in your life. You only have to develop some skill over time to begin to effectively manage stress, prevent stress from becoming distress, and to begin enjoying an improved quality of life! We wish you a great deal of success and encouragement on this journey.

Chapter 11

What Is Self-Care?

*Self-care is an act of self-respect and self-nurturing
that over time becomes a life-enhancing habit.*

—Dana Gionta

What is self-care you may wonder? Self-care is a gift we give ourselves and others. It is an essential component of good stress management. At its simplest, self-care is the act of caring for our Self.

Many of us are very good at caring for others. We feel very good about doing so and invest many hours each day and week in doing so. We even take pride in how well we care for, and are there for, those we love, whether physically, emotionally, financially, or professionally. However, when it comes to truly caring for ourselves, we often find it very difficult—seemingly unnatural, one might add. We find it difficult to find the time to commit to it on a regular basis, to get family and friends' support, and even to figure out where to begin. I (Dana) know because I've also had similar feelings and experiences about taking care of my Self. My desire in writing this book is to share with you my hard-learned wisdom and lessons about what good self-care is, its essential components, and what it is not. It has made an invaluable difference in my life and for all of those I've had the privilege of working with over the years.

One of the greatest lessons I've learned is that good self-care is the foundation of, and the starting point for, transformative change in one's life. It doesn't matter what area of your life you're not happy with and would like to improve, either slightly or radically. Taking better care of your Self will begin the process of positive change and eventually could lead to a transformative life change, if that is what you desire.

The extraordinary and surprising thing about practicing good self-care is that it doesn't just benefit you in that one area; it trickles over into other areas of your life (like the scattering of a flower blossom's seeds). Before you know it, what began as a dance class to lose weight has become a source of increased energy (nice benefit also) and enjoyment—that which gives you joy. Perhaps you will even discover a hidden talent you never knew you had or something you now find yourself unexpectedly passionate about. That's exciting! This in turn leads to you feeling better about your body and gaining increased confidence in your discovered abilities. Also, you'll find you now have more energy, which makes keeping up with all your responsibilities a bit easier. Surprisingly, you will have the energy to begin or finally complete that project, go out with friends and socialize at night, or play with your children after dinner.

Self-Care and Others

Let me be clear: self-care isn't simply about taking a dance class or eating healthy meals five out of seven nights. That's a great start, however. I consider self-care to be a long-term lifestyle approach to how you live your life. It is something you do on a regular, consistent basis, and it becomes an integral part of your life. It encompasses activities and habits you do (saying no, doing something relaxing, engaging in a hobby) and don't do (overextending yourself, permitting others to treat you poorly, overeating) that maintain and support your well-being.

Self-care is also about the decisions and daily choices we make. Will this decision or choice enhance our emotional, physical, mental, spiritual, or financial well-being? What effect may it have on the quality of our relationships with family and friends? Decisions that support our self-care almost always improve our relationships with loved ones. The critical point here is that often it may take place over time, not immediately. When we make increased efforts to take care of ourselves, initially family and friends may find the noticed changes (new hairstyle, new wardrobe, the word "no" coming from your mouth) a bit threatening. There are various reasons for this that I will discuss later in this chapter. Despite their initial resistance, if you stay the course and continue following through with whatever self-care changes you are making, you will begin to notice loved ones coming around and being more supportive. Others might even begin saying how good you look (more confident, peaceful, happy) and ask what you have been doing. They may even start taking better care of themselves through your positive example and role modeling.

Before we go any further, you may have noticed that I am using a capital "S" in many words beginning with "self," or that I separate the word "yourself" into "your Self." I have intentionally done this to emphasize the importance of considering one's Self, and to create a different lens in which to view your Self. At times, I may also capitalize the word "You." This is also for emphasis, like I might do if we were talking together.

The Myth and Misconception About Self-Care

Can you guess what the most common misconception is about self-care? OK, going once, twice, times up! The most common misconception is that people who take good care of themselves are, oh no—one of the most feared words to be called—the "S word."

Get ready, you better sit down, it's . . . it's . . . "SELFISH," the horror! Have you fallen off your chair? I know, it's that dreaded "S-word," almost as dreaded as the "B-word" for women to be called. I am old enough now to have been called both; unfortunately, however, I wasn't that old when I heard both directed at me. The reality is that it can feel awful to be called either one—shaming, embarrassing, like you've committed a crime. What I have observed over the years, both personally and professionally, is that you are often called these names when you are doing something or making a choice that is good for your Self and goes against others' and society's expectations.

What is most important to know is that self-care is not selfish. Self-care is showing respect and consideration for your Self. It is self-consideration. You are worth it, and so are those you love. By practicing good self-care, you will bring your better self into any relationship.

The Numerous Benefits of Good Self-Care

There are many visible and subtle short- and long-term benefits to investing in your Self with good self-care. I use the word "investment" because that's exactly what it is. It takes time, planning, effort, commitment, and periodic re-evaluations to maintain or get back on track and assess your progress. However, your health, emotional well-being, happiness, and quality of your relationships are worth it.

Clear and Visible Benefits

You will feel and look more peaceful.

You will experience less stress.

You will have more energy.

You will be more mentally present for those you love.

You will appear more self-confident, acting with greater self-respect.

Subtle Benefits

Improved concentration

Improved health

Increased time to do what you would like

Increased sense of control

All of these benefits, taken individually, are valuable. However, they often have what we call synergistic effects where they build upon and enhance each other. For example, your increased energy levels will allow you to be more present with and for those you love, and to react less and respond better to them. This in turn will improve the quality of your relationships with your loved ones. They will experience the difference in you. They in turn will respond more positively and calmly to you, which will have other benefits.

A Glimpse into What Self-Care Is Not: Unhealthy Coping Strategies

There are many ways we try to cope with increasing stress levels and demands on our time, energy, and patience. The unfortunate part of this is that many times the exact things we do to attempt to reduce our stress and make us feel better actually end up increasing our stress levels, both in the short term and long term. It's like eating that supposedly nutritious frozen entree and finding out that it had hydrogenated oils, hardly any protein, and 800 mg of sodium. It's pretty frustrating and confusing, I know. So, this is very similar to what happens with some of the coping strategies we engage in to manage our stress levels or to deal with everything that is tossed on our plates (if we allow that to happen).

Examples of Unhealthy Coping Strategies

Overeating or Under Eating

Oversleeping or Under Sleeping

Drinking

Gambling

Smoking

Drug use

Withdrawal, Isolation Behaviors

Blame/Rage

Shopping

Avoidance, Procrastination

Yours? _____

None of the above behaviors address the stressor directly or effectively or enhance your well-being in any way. It may seem like it *in the moment*; however, shortly afterward, such behaviors often lead to increased feelings of guilt, blame, and anger directed at yourself. This makes you feel bad about yourself. Such behaviors often result in stress coming back to you, often in increased amounts, not reduced amounts, and this makes it harder, not easier, to cope with whatever situation you have. For example, avoiding a problem often leads to the situation getting worse or what we call a "pileup of stressors" not being addressed.

Anything you do that goes against your values, goals, or promises to your Self, that You believe you shouldn't be doing, or anything that is negatively affecting others and/or yourself, is *not* self-care.

You and Your Self-Care: Where Are You Now?

Our Self-Care Inventory

Let's take a moment and assess your current level of self-care. Please carefully read each question on the following self-care inventory. Think of a typical week for you within the past month and answer true or false as honestly as you can.

1. Everyday, I do something good for myself. _____

2. My energy level is consistently moderate to high. _____

3. I do something healthy for myself each day. _____

4. I exercise regularly three to five times per week. _____

5. I generally eat what I consider to be healthy meals daily (including fruits and vegetables, and small to moderate portion sizes). _____

6. I am able to set boundaries with others when I need to do so. _____

7. I schedule my health check ups (doctor, dentist, dermatology) in the recommended time frame. _____

8. I feel quite productive in general. _____

9. I feel I regularly practice good self-care each week. _____

10. I and others would say my mood is most often upbeat and positive. _____

11. I feel happy with my life. _____

12. I often feel overwhelmed in my life. _____

13. I typically feel drained at the end of the day. _____

14. I notice myself crying unexpectedly, and often over little things. _____

15. Finding time for myself each day is a real struggle. _____

16. I typically feel moderate to high levels of stress each week. _____

17. I am finding it harder each week to make time on a regular basis for my own healthy or enjoyable activities. _____

18. I find myself doing my self-care practices (exercising, eating healthy, enjoyable hobby, socializing with friends, meditation/journaling) less consistently as the weeks go by. _____

19. I used to exercise three to five times a week, and I notice lately I'm doing it only one to two times a week. _____

20. I feel weighed down by my responsibilities. _____

21. I would say I more often squeeze in time for myself, if the week allows. _____

22. I schedule me-time each week, as I would an important appointment. _____

23. I think my self-care has been slipping over the past month or two. _____

24. There is one or more relationships in my life that I find quite stressful, like a roller coaster, at times. _____

25. I often feel like I have no control in my life. _____

26. I find myself drinking more alcohol throughout the week. _____

27. I typically do something fun each week. _____

28. I am having difficulty falling or staying asleep. _____

29. I feel like I am often worried about money. _____

30. I notice myself eating more sweets and carbs over the past few weeks. _____

Interpretation of Scores

Now that you've taken our self-care inventory, let's take a look at your self-evaluated stress level.

Q. 1–11; 22; 27: If you answer "true" to the majority of these questions (at least ten of the thirteen items), this is a good indicator that you are regularly practicing good self-care and that your overall stress level is in the low range. You are what we consider in the green zone. You will learn more about what being in the green zone means in Chapter 13.

Q. 17–21; 23; 29–30: If you answer "true" to the majority of these questions (at least five items of eight), your self-care behaviors are occurring less consistently, which is an indicator that you are likely experiencing more moderate levels of stress.

Q. 12–16; 24–26; 28: If you answer "true" to the majority of these questions (at least five items of nine), this is an indicator that your self-care behaviors have most likely decreased significantly and that your stress level is in the high range. You are in the red zone.

Note: If you answer true to at least five items in the moderate stress level range (yellow zone) and also five items in the high stress level range (red zone), consider your current stress level to be in the *high* range.

First, congratulate your Self for making the time to complete this inventory! If You are happy with your score, that is wonderful. Keep doing what you are doing, and consider adding one or two practices or tips from our book to your current self-care routine. If you scored in the yellow or red zone, that is very valuable information that you have just discovered about yourself.

You now have the opportunity and choice to make some small lifestyle changes to take better care of your Self, and increase your resilience to stress! In Chapter 13, we will discuss further what being in the green, yellow, and red zones mean. Let's get started. ☺

Life Priorities

Please list your top five priorities in your life currently (list the most important first, then next in importance, and so on, if you can):

1. _____

2. _____

3. _____

4. _____

5. _____

Reflection Exercise

Review your responses above, and observe where you put your Self on your list of priorities, if at all! Congratulations if you did include yourself on the list! This was a bit tricky of me, so don't get too disappointed if you didn't. Now, reflect on where you put your Self on the list and what led you to place yourself higher or lower. Ask yourself, "Is this where I'd like to stay?

If so, why?

_____

_____

_____

If not, why not?

_____

_____

_____

What might you begin doing to make your Self more of a priority?

_____

_____

_____

_____

If you are nowhere to be found on the list, then consider how not making yourself a priority might be affecting your well-being, relationships, or happiness.

Identify two or three ways it might be affecting you:

1. _____

2. _____

3. _____

Imagine you went to bed and were visited by a genie. The two of you had a heart to heart conversation, and the genie shared with you how you could begin to make yourself a priority.

What did the genie say to you?

_____

_____

_____

_____

_____

_____

_____

_____

_____

Chapter 12

Creating Your Self-Care Toolkit

When the well's dry, we know the worth of water.

—Benjamin Franklin

Your self-care toolkit is for everyday use as well as for those especially stressful weeks. We definitely don't want to leave it on the shelf and let dust pile up, like our stress levels! If we assume we have a regular self-care routine that is working well for us, the toolkit becomes a valuable resource for those weeks or periods in our lives when we feel particularly stressed. For example, you are dealing with a demanding project at work for the next three weeks, your child is having increased difficulty at school, or your parent is having health issues (i.e., fell), and you need to re-arrange your schedule to care-give. All of these examples are typical for many individuals, families, and employees, each of which can result in significant increases in our stress. It is during periods of increased stress that we need to increase, not reduce, our self-care behaviors. This is a critical factor in managing our stress well. The self-care toolbox makes this easier because we can refer to it and add to our self-care routine during these stressful times.

There are several elements that are an essential part of any good self-care toolkit. We will start with the three pillars:

1. Healthy nutrition

2. Regular exercise

3. Consistent and sufficient sleep

Other key tools are emotional, spiritual, and physical renewal (e.g., mental health days); supportive positive relationships; enjoyable hobbies/social life; spiritual practices; prioritizing laughter, fun, and play in your life; regular medical check-ups; financial health (feeling in control); and a healthy workplace environment.

Nutrition, Exercise, and Sleep: The Three Pillars

Despite how much time, energy, and advertising dollars are spent in these three areas, we believe the importance of healthy nutrition, regular exercise, and consistent and sufficient sleep cannot be overstated. For the purposes of this section, we are more interested in addressing what gets in the way of having some success in these areas than we are in simply telling you that you need this!

Pillar #1: Nutrition

We all hear repeatedly how important it is to eat healthy. We know intellectually that we should eat better—more fruits and vegetables, less fat and processed foods . . . blah, blah, blah—this is exactly what often happens. We begin to tune out those relentless messages especially if we find ourselves not following them. We don't want to be reminded that we're failing, not taking very good care of ourselves, and perhaps not taking care of our families either. So, considering this, we are not going to share here what you've heard before hundreds of times. We promise!

Nutrition is not dieting. It is not about eating perfectly, and it does not mean taking the joy out of eating. One way to think about nutrition is in terms of our energy: nutrition = energy. When we eat well, we have more energy, feel better physically and psychologically, think and focus more clearly, and can more easily maintain or even lose weight. Our skin also often looks better. Another way to think about nutrition is to see it like providing the proper nutrients to a garden so the plants and flowers can grow and thrive.

With so many benefits of healthy nutrition, why is it still so challenging for us to eat right? There are many reasons. We'll list just a few.

Challenges to Eating Healthy

Stress

As our stress levels go up, so do our cravings for comfort food, carbohydrates, and sweets. This is because stress increases our cortisol levels and decreases our serotonin levels. Serotonin serves to curve our cravings, so as serotonin levels go down and cortisol levels go up, our desire for comfort food and carbs increases (Shaar & Britton, 2011).

Occasional indulgences we know are fine. However, if we find ourselves really stressed, we might be indulging daily or three to four times per week. We might even find ourselves beginning to have multiple glasses of wine or beer to relax and unwind. Unfortunately, what feels good in the short term—comfort food, carbs, and alcohol—actually leads to *increased* stress levels. For example, we may notice ourselves gaining weight, feeling more lethargic, and being less productive. After noticing these changes in ourselves, our stress levels often go up. Many of us then try to compensate for the reduced energy. We do this by drinking more coffee or soda to get a caffeine boost—to increase our energy levels—or by turning to chocolate or sweets to get a sugar boost. You've been found out! ☺ Either way, both are unhealthy in the moderate to long run, and they put us on an energy roller coaster.

What about alcohol? Many of us believe alcohol, in the short run, can help us feel more relaxed and calmer, with fewer worries. However, alcohol, for many people, can cause a feeling of increased anxiety and uneasiness beginning from twenty-four hours up to seventy-two hours after drinking. This occurs at times because alcohol changes our blood sugar levels and increases our heart rate. This may contribute to a rebound experience of anxiety.

Convenience

Junk food is often more easily accessible (via vending machines and fast food restaurants) than healthier alternatives. Besides just convenience, access to junk food is often quick and also inexpensive. We have less time and energy and more responsibilities than ever before, and sometimes it seems easier and more efficient to eat the less healthy alternatives. Going for the quick fix also appears to be a good and immediate short-term solution. However, in the long term there can be a significant cost to our health, which is often difficult for us to identify.

Family Influences

Family values, culture, and dynamics can have a powerful influence on our decisions around nutrition. These decisions include factors like what types of food we bring into the household, how meals are prepared, and how often we eat. For example, in your household, you may be the decision maker for buying the food, while another person in your family may be responsible for preparing it. Your role in the family often determines the level of accessibility and choice with regard to nutrition.

Family dynamics also influence our choices around eating. An example of a popular family dynamic is the relatives who come to visit and stock your house with delicious, fattening treats (and sometimes then tell you that you're putting on some weight!). In this instance, it would be difficult not to indulge in these tempting treats both on the level of honoring their generosity and our cravings.

Work Schedule

In this era of doing more in a shorter amount of time, we may feel too tired when we come home from work to cook something healthy. Our tendency is to then grab fast food on the way home, skimp on meals with a bowl of cereal, or even settle for chips or popcorn. Another example is when we are late for work: we may run out the door in the morning without having any breakfast at all. Working through lunch is another increasingly common practice that often leads to poorer food choices or eating behaviors (i.e., overeating, eating quickly) later in the day.

Easy Tips for Better Nutrition

Start by replacing one or two small items a day with ones that are healthier for you (i.e., milk instead of half-and-half in your coffee, a side salad instead of fries with your burger) or by adding in new foods that would be healthy for you (i.e., avocados, fish high in omega-3s, or shiitake mushrooms). Try to avoid skipping meals throughout your day and eat without multitasking.

Pillar #2: Exercise

There is so much to say on this subject. Most of us know that exercise is necessary and good for our health. When we exercise, we often feel better, gain more energy, have a more positive outlook, concentrate more easily, have less stress, enjoy better sex, sleep better, and eat healthier. There is not much dispute there. What many of us may not know is that exercise does not have to take loads of time, demand unreasonable amounts of effort, or require you to participate in traditional modes of exercise in order to get results. Following three simple rules (1) move your body, (2) do more that you are currently doing, and (3) be consistent, not resistant can help anyone (and we mean anyone) start and maintain an effective exercise program.

Move Your Body

Exercise does not have to be going to the gym or running around a track. The key is to find something you enjoy doing, give yourself permission to take the time to do it, and make exercise and yourself a priority!

Climb stairs

Dance (salsa dancing is one of Dana's favorites!)

Do yoga (Hatha yoga is one of Dan's favorites!)

Hike in the mountains

Jump on a trampoline

Lift and lower your arms to music

Mall walk

Play sports

Roller-skate

Ski/Snowboard

Stretch

Surf

Swim

Walk on the beach

What exercises are you currently doing that you enjoy, if any?

_____

_____

_____

_____

_____

What exercises might you enjoy that you have not yet tried?

_____

_____

_____

_____

PHYSIOLOGICAL BENEFITS OF EXERCISE

Boosts your metabolism, aiding you to achieve and maintain a healthier weight

Lowers your blood pressure and cholesterol

Controls your blood sugar

Improves your sleep

Allows your skin to look healthier

Improves your digestive system

Lifts your mood

Increases your energy and slows gravity

Raises your serotonin levels, making you feel calmer and more upbeat. Yay!

Decreases your cortisol levels, lowering your stress levels and reducing your cravings. This, in turn, helps you make healthier food choices. Another Yay!

As you can see, exercise is an integral part of good self-care, and one of the three pillars because of the numerous benefits.

Do More Than You Are Currently Doing

This requires an honest assessment of how much activity you are doing now and thinking about what small adjustment you could make to do more. Here are some examples: If currently you only walk from your house to the car and from your car parking lot to the office, you may consider trying to park a little further from the home or the office. If you typically exercise two times per week, consider increasing it to three times per week. Consider starting your morning by stretching or exercising for five to ten minutes before eating breakfast or jumping into the shower. Here is another: Combine your goal of spending more time with your family with your goal of a regular walk through the neighborhood or a local park one to three times per week. Now you have a successful base to work with.

Several years ago, I (Dana) found it quite hard to get started exercising, in essence, to do more than I was currently doing and then to stick with it. Then it hit me: I'm awake sixteen to seventeen hours a day, so how am I not able to find twenty to thirty minutes several times a week to exercise? How come I could not find time to *invest* in my physical and emotional well-being? Could I afford to continue *not* exercising? One of the best investments I made was buying a treadmill, so now I can exercise whenever I want. Whatever you need to do, do it to invest in your health. You are worth it!

Be Consistent, Not Resistant

This simply means that the focus is on purposeful, planned days and times that you choose to exercise. It may be tempting to choose an amount of time and frequency that you believe you *should* be exercising, but you may later find out that you are resistant to this because of busyness, tiredness, or lack of motivation. In our opinion, it is important when first starting an exercise routine to choose a length and frequency of time that guarantees success (yes, we are asking you to *undershoot* at first). The best way to shortcut resistance is by choosing a realistic plan that allows you to be consistent and successful!

Earlier in the chapter, you listed forms of exercise that you might enjoy doing. Let's set an exercise goal that will set you up to succeed.

What is the minimum number of times and minutes per week you could do your chosen form of exercise and be consistent?

Type of Exercise? _____

Number of times? _____

How long? _____

Pillar #3: Sleep

Sleep is an integral component of good self-care. Insufficient sleep can lead to a host of related issues including afternoon cravings; energy-boosting efforts (caffeine, sweets); reduced concentration and memory lapses; feelings of being overwhelmed; increased irritability; lowered immune system, resulting in more frequent colds; and weight gain. Research has shown that people who are sleep-deprived have more trouble resisting high-fat and high-sugar foods (Shaar & Britton, 2011).

Many of us are not aware of how important sleep is to our well-being. It is important to remember that you are not a human doing, but a human being. Part of being human is the non-doing, what is sometimes called the "ground" of being. Science has still not figured out precisely why we need sleep, but it has figured out that without proper sleep, our human systems go haywire. Attending to our sleep is attending to the "being" part of our humanness. Using a transportation metaphor, it is the difference between driving on roads and highways filled with obstacles and potholes (poor sleep) vs. driving on ones that are freshly paved, open, and very navigable (good sleep).

Alcohol and Sleep

What is the relationship between alcohol and sleep? Although having two or three glasses of wine or beer may first appear to relax us and help us fall asleep, it also has the less well-known effect of interrupting our sleep in the middle of the night, resulting in a less restful sleep. If you drink alcohol daily, then each night you are likely experiencing interrupted sleep that is adversely affecting the quality of your sleep. To minimize the effects of alcohol on your sleep, we suggest avoiding consumption of any alcohol at least three hours prior to bedtime and cutting down on the overall amount and frequency of alcohol each week (Mann, 2013).

Easy Tips for Better Sleep

Prepare for sleep in the following ways:

1. Take a warm bath or shower before bed.

2. Turn off all televisions, computers, video games, smartphones, and other mind-stimulating devices forty-five minutes before bedtime. You may choose to listen to soothing music, read something light and relaxing (not news), pray, meditate, or lightly stretch.

3. Avoid talking with anyone by telephone who is frequently argumentative, demanding, or problem-focused before bedtime.

4. Avoid reading email on your smartphone or computer before bedtime. You can also charge those devices out of your bedroom to prevent being woken up by audible notifications of texts, emails, or calls, or to prevent being tempted to check those devices during the night.

5. Pay attention to, and be creative in, modifying your sleeping environment to fit your needs. Examples of this include using ear plugs, a white noise machine or a fan if you live in a noisy environment/city, buying dark curtains so no morning light comes through, using a humidifier or dehumidifier to create your best sleeping atmosphere, and sampling different mattresses.

6. Drink a cup of decaffeinated, herbal tea like chamomile or jasmine tea with a spoonful of wild, raw honey. Alternatively,

try a glass of warm milk (with or without the honey).

Are you getting enough sleep? If not, take some time to ask yourself, and journal about, what is making it difficult to get a good night's rest.

Do I get seven to eight hours of sleep a night?

_____

Are my sleep problems temporary or long-standing?

_____

_____

What factors can I control to allow myself to get more sleep?

_____

_____

_____

_____

What things can I do this week to improve my sleep?

_____

_____

_____

_____

What is the wonderful connection between all three pillars? When we eat healthier, we have more energy to exercise. In turn, the exercise helps us sleep better over time! Sufficient sleep reduces cravings and regenerates the body after exercise, making it easier to eat healthier and exercise again and again! This creates a positive feedback loop that brings us full circle. ☺

Other Tools in Our Self-Care Toolkit

Renewal (emotional/mental/spiritual/physical)

We all need to regularly renew these important areas of our overall well-being. If we don't, we will begin to feel emotionally or mentally overwhelmed, spiritually disconnected, and physically drained. Renewal can take many forms and is often very individual. What really rejuvenates and relaxes one person may have a very different effect on another. It is important to take your time and identify what really helps relax and renew you. For example, spending time at the beach or listening to country music may work wonders for you, however, your friend hates sand, and wouldn't be caught dead listening to country music; therefore, that's probably not what she would choose to restore her emotionally, mentally, or spiritually.

To prevent your stress level escalating to the point where you feel you have to take time off from work, periodically giving yourself permission to take a day off from work can be one effective way of renewing your emotional health. Other considerations include taking an overnight mini-vacation or weekend away; giving yourself permission to do nothing for a day/weekend; disconnecting from all technology or people; participating in a retreat; spending a day at a spa; going hiking in the mountains; watching hours of old movies, "I Love Lucy" episodes, or your favorite sitcom. The key is to do what is unique to *you*, that helps you relax, feel more peaceful, and lifts your spirits, and to do it consistently, not once or twice a year.

An important warning sign is a feeling of complete exhaustion that lasts more than a few weeks. If you are not able to feel renewed after doing what has in the past been very effective, you may be experiencing emotional, mental, or physical burnout. Burnout needs to be taken seriously, and we recommend that you seek professional help.

KEY SIGNS OF BURNOUT

To determine whether you might be experiencing symptoms of burnout, or are at risk of burnout in the near future, review the following key signs below, adapted from an article published by the Institute for Quality and Efficiency in Health Care (IQWiG) (2013).

Emotional exhaustion: You feel drained and exhausted, over-loaded, tired and low, and do not have enough energy.

Alienation from (job-related) activities: People affected find their jobs increasingly negative and frustrating. They may develop a cynical attitude toward their work environment and their colleagues. They may at the same time increasingly distance themselves emotionally and disengage themselves from their work.

Reduced performance: Burnout mainly affects everyday tasks at work, at home, or when caring for family members. People with burnout regard their activities very negatively, find it hard to concentrate, are listless, and experience a lack of creativity.

Hobbies/Social Life

Cultivating hobbies that we like or are passionate about, and making time to do them on a regular basis, is an important component of good self-care. Regularly doing something that we enjoy lifts our spirits and our energy, relaxes us, releases our stress, broadens our perspective (i.e., life can be fun), and expands our social circle and support system. These are all very positive benefits toward taking care of ourselves!

If you already do some activity that you enjoy weekly or more frequently, then commend yourself and keep it up. If you don't, or are not sure where to begin because you don't know what you like, then consider embarking on an adventure of self-discovery or an experiment of sorts.

Start exploring different hobbies, sports, and social activities that you might find interesting. Reflect on what you enjoyed as a child. You might still love doing that but not know it. Don't let fear or embarrassment stop you. You might be amazed at what you discover about yourself. For example, for years I was quite afraid (I admit it) to go parasailing, mostly because of how high it looked, how thin the rope seemed, and the possibility of a crash landing. None of which seemed appealing. Then, one summer, I decided to face my fear and explore the possibility of actually going. I signed up to go and gave myself permission to sit on the boat and observe. If it looked safe and doable, I would go up. If not, at least I took one step toward confronting my fear and attempting something I always thought it must be a magical, extraordinary experience. I wanted to fly as a child, and I always admired and fantasized about what it must be like to be a bird. This was the closest I was going to get (unless I confront my next fear: skydiving). The greatest lesson I learned that day on the beach was that so much of my fear was based on the unknown, what I had *imagined* parasailing was like (e.g., a hard landing on the boat), not the reality of the experience. I am happy to say I took flight, and it proved to be an amazing, breathtakingly beautiful experience. Although I will not do this activity regularly, it is something I have promised myself I will do as often as I can.

Is there some activity or sport you have secretly wanted to do but have let fear stop you from trying? My gift to you is try it, risk it—and possibly discover how courageous, talented, and capable you are. Nothing builds confidence better than confronting our fears!

Spiritual Practices

Honoring our spirituality, however we conceive it to be and whatever form it takes for us (i.e., being in nature, with animals, with God, in prayer, in meditation, or doing yoga), is an important part of taking care of ourselves. Making time and space to connect to our spirit is so important as it ultimately serves to connect us to ourselves. Through this connection, we get to know ourselves—our feelings, needs, dreams, values, nature—at a deeper level.

Give yourself permission to make time for your spiritual practices. You will experience greater peace, new perspectives, and increased presence over time. It will happen subtly, and likely without you noticing the changes, as most personal growth does!

Prioritizing Laughter, Fun, and Play

This is so important and a critical part of good self-care. When we're younger, playing and having fun comes naturally. There's no need to think about it, let alone plan it. It's also expected and accepted as part of being a child or young adult. Somewhere along the line we come to believe that playing and having fun is for children. Another belief is that we don't have time to have fun or be playful. We may have time, but believe play is not a responsible use of our time. All of these beliefs lead to the same outcome: we don't make time for fun.

Play is not a priority for most of us. We think we can't have fun until we've done everything else we need to do and our to-do list is completely checked off. Only then can we can give ourselves permission to do something that we enjoy.

Some people have never lost their playful, fun-loving personalities. They continue to make play a priority in their lives and can't see any other way to live their lives. Following their example is a great way to practice good self-care because of the numerous benefits fun and laughter have on our health and well-being overall.

So what do you do on a daily and weekly basis to have fun? If you cannot think of anything you are currently doing, then reflect back and think of activities that you used to do that were fun.

List your fun activities here:

_____

_____

_____

_____

_____

Financial Health

Financial health can significantly affect our emotions and our physical health. If we feel financially comfortable, are able to pay our key expenses and have something left for enjoyment and savings, we experience a greater peace of mind, security, confidence in one's self, and often a feeling of success. When we do not have sufficient money, and are not able to, or are just barely making ends meet, there is often much daily worry, future anxiety, stress, fear, helplessness, and perhaps feelings of failure and shame. Experiencing these negative emotions on a frequent basis is not healthy for us, especially over the long term. Chronic worry can and often does weigh us down, making it difficult to focus on and enjoy the good in our life. Whatever we can do to improve our financial situation, to feel in control, and to live more within our means, the better we will feel—emotionally, mentally, and physically. Taking care of our finances is also key to attending to our well-being, and an important component of good self-care.

Seek support and professional guidance with your finances if you believe you are living above your means or feel overwhelmed with your financial situation. Do your best not to judge yourself, just commit to improving your situation, one step at a time. There are caring professionals with specialized training to help you. Do whatever research you need to feel comfortable and to make an informed decision. Consider getting several referrals and interviewing each before making a final decision.

Medical Health

Part of good self-care also involves our own physical maintenance and regular medical check-ups, screenings, and cleanings. As we get older, this becomes even more important, and possibly more challenging, because we're so busy with work, household, childrearing, community, and caregiving responsibilities.

Again, think of regular physical maintenance as an investment in you, your future, and your family, so you will be healthy and fit for years to come, sharing quality time and fun activities with those important to you. If you have children, this is even more relevant. I find it helpful to associate these checkups with important dates in your life to make it easier to remember. For example, I like to schedule my physical exam during the month of my birthday, or as close to it as possible. For fun, you can schedule your dental cleaning after Halloween, knowing you likely indulged in the treat part quite generously. Consider also scheduling these checkups around the same time each year so it becomes almost routine, making them easier to remember. By doing this, you free yourself from worrying that you haven't done it yet, you need to go, you should make the appointment, what if something is wrong, etc. All of these subtle reminders create undue stress, worry, and distractions, which takes away from peace of mind, energy, and presence with loved ones. As you invest in yourself this way, you will feel more in control, confident, and proud of yourself. Isn't that worth it?

Healthy Workplace Environment

One of the potentially greatest sources of stress for us is our work. Sixty-nine percent of employees report that work is a significant source of stress and 41 percent say they typically feel tense or stressed out during the workday (American Psychological Association, 2009). However, only 36 percent of Americans say their organizations provide sufficient resources to help them manage stress (American Psychological Association, 2013b). An important aspect of whether we feel our job or career is stressful is the nature of the environment we work in. This includes both the physical environment and the emotional climate and culture of our workplace—within our department, unit, or team and organization as a whole. Do we feel our office/work environment is physically safe, clean, and without health hazards (e.g., asbestos)? Safety is a basic need and standard everyone has and deserves. How is the emotional climate? Is it a supportive, friendly, caring environment, with teamwork and camaraderie and open, direct communication? Or is morale low, attitudes negative or pessimistic, gossip prevalent, criticism and fault-finding/blaming frequent, tempers permitted, and expectations unspoken?

A healthy, supportive, positive work environment will contribute to your feeling calm, positive, appreciated, and cared for. You will generally look forward to going to work and spending the day with your coworkers and boss. Even if your actual work is somewhat stressful or the clients/customers you deal with are challenging, having your work environment safe, supportive, and healthy makes a tremendous difference in being able to deal with these other work stressors.

If you find yourself feeling tense and anxious, dread going to the office, or have developed unexplained health symptoms (e.g., headaches, stomach aches, sleep issues, neck/shoulder tightness, chest palpitations, or other discomfort), your work environment or job might be compromising your emotional and physical health. Depending on the duration and intensity of the above symptoms, this may be a toxic work situation for you. If you are unsure or suspect this may be the case, consider speaking to a health professional regarding this. You may want to explore other work options as well, such as transitioning to another department within your company, making a lateral move to another company or changing your line of work all together. You and your well-being are worth evaluating the health of your work environment, and making a change if it is not healthy!

Good self-care is working in an environment and at a position that feels positive, supportive, and enjoyable in general. There are always trying situations, and weeks that bring more stress than others; however, these times should be short term and occasional, not typical. Your body and emotions will always tell you the truth. Just listen.

FACTORS CONTRIBUTING TO EMPLOYEE WORK LIFE SATISFACTION

Being energized by work and finding it meaningful, as well as having a supportive supervisor, working for an organization that values work-life balance and having control over whether or not to do work-related activities during non-work hours play major roles in how satisfied an employee is with his or her work life and how well it fits with other life demands (American Psychological Association, 2013a).

Chapter 13

When to Use Your Self-Care Toolkit

The time to relax is when you don't have time for it.

—Sydney J. Harris

You're probably wondering why there's a particular chapter about this, correct? I knew it! Either you're thinking, we should *always* use our self-care toolkit, or we should use it when we're feeling stressed. It's true that we definitely want to practice several of our self-care behaviors (in our toolkit) on a regular basis. We can think of the toolkit then as something to take out (and hopefully not dust off) when we are experiencing an unusually stressful few days, week, or period in our life (i.e., caring for an ill family member, balancing financial difficulties, managing work stress). It is during these times that we want to include additional self-care practices in our normal self-care routine to help offset the more intense level of stress that we're experiencing. The irony is that it is exactly during periods of increased stress that we often tell ourselves that we don't have time for our self-care because of these extra demands. Although counter-intuitive, it is during such times that we most need to practice good self-care!

In order to do this, we need to know when we're experiencing increased stress. One would think this is pretty easy. Now, feeling like we're going to lose our minds is a sure sign of over-the-top stress. However, we don't want our stress to get to this point! An important question is, how good are we in knowing how much stress we're really under?

Until I became aware of what I like to call "'tolerance" to stress, I thought I was pretty good at assessing my level of stress, especially as a psychologist. After several memorable experiences, I realized that something was happening that made it difficult to accurately assess how stressed I really was. One such experience was taking a vacation, and getting away from all my professional and personal demands for a week.

It wasn't until I was away, and out of my everyday environment, that I realized for the first time the high level of stress I had been under. I found this concerning to say the least, and I realized I needed to make some important changes.

So what is it that happens? It is the phenomena of what I call "tolerance" to stress. The concept of tolerance to stress appears misleading. Tolerance to stress refers to the very subtle process of adapting emotionally to our environment. Often, we come to believe that we are better able to handle the increasing demands on our time and energy. What we once found quite stressful, we believe we've adapted to, are able to handle, and are no longer bothered by. Unfortunately, this is not true for most of us. A nice illustration of this concept is the "frog in a boiling pot" metaphor. If we put a frog in a boiling pot of water, it knows immediately to jump out and save his little froggy body. If, however, we put the same frog in a pot of warm water and slowly over time raise the temperature, the frog doesn't recognize what is happening, since the change in his environment is slow and subtle, until it's too late. This is what happens to many of us.

You might be wondering right about now: Am I that frog? Is this happening to me, but I don't realize it? We don't want this to continue to happen to any of us.

Assess Your Stress: Green, Yellow, and Red Zone

In order to prevent this from happening, we need to learn how to more accurately assess our level of stress. One of the best ways I have discovered to determine stress levels is by paying careful attention to self-care practices. Using our self-care practices as a gauge, we can assess our stress level to be in one of three zones: green, yellow, or red.

Green Zone

When life is going along relatively smoothly, you don't feel stressed, and you're able to consistently maintain your daily and weekly self-care behaviors with relative ease (i.e., exercise, read a book, socialize with friends, play with your children or pets), then your stress level is in the green zone. This indicates that your overall level of stress is quite low, in the 1–3 range on a scale of 1–10.

Yellow Zone

In this zone, you are maintaining *most* of your self-care behaviors. However, it is becoming more difficult, and you notice that some of your regular self-care practices are beginning to slip (i.e., your exercise has dropped from three to two days per week; you haven't played with your children/pets in days; your socializing with your partner or friends have been rescheduled multiple times). You are also aware that you have been experiencing some symptoms of stress lately.

Your stress level has now reached the yellow zone. A stress level in the yellow zone indicates a low to moderate level of stress, in the 4–6 range on a scale of 1–10. This is an indicator to pay increased attention. Demands in your work, family, or personal life have increased. When your routine self-care behaviors begin to slip, it is a sign that you are likely experiencing increased demands.

If you don't attend to your stress and resume your routine self-care behaviors, over time your stress level will increase, and you will move into the red zone.

Red Zone

Your stress level is in the red zone when you realize most, if not all, of your typical self-care practices have disappeared from your regular routine and occur more by chance. For example, you notice that you haven't done anything for your self—you haven't been to the gym or spent quality time with friends or family in weeks or months. It may take two to three months before you notice something has changed, unless you're really paying attention. When your stress level is in the red zone (range of 7–10), you will definitely notice yourself feeling greater stress for an extended period of time. If you don't take action and make immediate changes at this time, you are on your way to becoming the boiled frog. It's important to know that unaddressed red zone stress levels can over time have serious effects on your health (see Chapter 2: Stress Indicators). So, you can think of this as a red alert to you, to stop everything and identify what has changed in your life. Ask yourself what new responsibilities or expectations have occurred in the past one to three months. Have there been any changes in your schedule that have added more work? Are you under greater pressure, either through external circumstances or self-imposed? Have there been any changes in the quality of your relationships—increased conflict, less emotional connection? These can all contribute to increased stress.

The goal is to practice regular self-care so the daily stressors (i.e., printer on the fritz) and more unexpected ones (i.e., conflict with a good friend) don't affect you as much because you're taking good care of yourself, emotionally and physically. These periods of increased stress—when you've identified that you're in the yellow or red zone—are the best times to use your self-care toolkit.

Seven Strategies for Managing Your Stress

First, identify the top two or three key stressors in your life.

Second, rate them on a scale of 1–10. Again, stressors in the range of 6–10 need both your *attention* and *intention* to take action to better manage this stressor.

Third, increase your self-care behaviors, especially if your stress is approaching the high range (7–10). This also can be considered a step you are taking!

Fourth, determine which stressors are under your control.

Fifth, shift your focus and your words to problem-solving mode —solutions—and *be proactive!*

Sixth, explore options and strategies to decrease or eliminate the stressors from your life, if possible.

Finally, work toward establishing a greater sense of control at home and at work, as we know perceived control, in general, will reduce your level of stress.

Chapter 14

Boundaries and You

True strength is found in standing firm, yet bending gently.

—Author unknown

A great way to increase our sense of control and reduce our stress is by setting boundaries.

What is a boundary, you ask, and why are they important? In essence, a boundary is a limit defining you in relationship to someone or to something. Boundaries can be physical and tangible or emotional and intangible. You may not be familiar with the "B" word, however, I (Dana) bet you have used and heard the concept of it before. If you have ever told someone that "I draw the line here," then you have already set a boundary! If you have informed someone that this is *your* office space, *your* desk or *your* designated chair (and who hasn't), you have attempted to set physical boundaries. Another clear example of a physical boundary is a fence, showing the border of our yard to our neighbors. It is often easier to understand a physical boundary. Emotional or mental boundaries may be a bit subtler; however, they are equally, if not more, important.

The Function of Boundaries

Boundaries serve many functions. They help to protect us, to clarify what is our responsibility and what is another's, to preserve our physical and emotional energy, to stay focused on ourselves, to live our values and standards, and to identify our personal limits.

Identifying, setting, and maintaining boundaries are skills—valuable skills that, unfortunately, we are often not taught either in school or in the workplace. If we have been fortunate enough to have learned to set good boundaries, it was likely through role models we had the opportunity to observe. Other ways we commonly learn boundary setting is through trial-and-error and hard-won experience.

Boundaries are essential to healthy relationships and a satisfying life. They are also instrumental in our ability to establish and maintain healthy work/life balance. We can apply them in any areas—our personal, professional, and family lives, and in the physical, emotional, spiritual, and financial domains.

Let's get a better understanding by reviewing personal situations that need boundaries.

Examples of Personal Situations Needing Boundaries

> Your sibling, roommate, or friend borrows your clothes, computer, or phone without asking.

> Your friend, family member, or coworker continue to share your confidences with others, which you do not like.

> You notice yourself frequently feeling very uncomfortable and anxious after watching or reading something that is violent or graphic.

> Your friends or extended family frequently call you during *known* special times (i.e., family dinner hours) or challenging times (i.e., just when you get home, during your children's bedtime routine), which leads you to feel stressed or resentful.

> Your friend or adult children often ask you for money and do not pay you back.

> Your partner or children frequently tell you how to drive or criticize your driving when you are in the car together.

> Your in-laws or friends often drop in on you without first asking if you have other plans. (Your plans might be to relax by yourself at home.)

Your family members talk disrespectfully toward you or express anger in ways that make you feel uncomfortable, hurt, or drained.

Your hair stylist of ten years continues to ignore your requests for a change, and you leave feeling frustrated and disappointed.

Everyone is sitting at the dinner table, interacting with their gadgets instead of each other.

Examples of Professional Situations that Warrant Boundaries

Your clients call you during known dinner hours or after ten o'clock at night when you requested they call you no later than seven o'clock.

You were recently hired for a position. After starting, you find yourself doing something completely different.

Your boss reprimands you repeatedly in front of your coworkers or clients.

You continue to receive office emails and phone calls while you are on vacation.

You are often asked to work during your lunch hour or in the evenings.

You had an agreement with your boss or client for a specific time frame or deadline date for a project and shortly afterward you receive requests to complete it earlier.

If you don't do exactly what your client wants (even if it's not in their best interest), he/she gets angry or threatens to go elsewhere with their business.

Your family/friends call you *throughout* the day at the office, after you repeatedly requested they call you at select times or only if urgent.

Understanding Boundaries

In this section I am going to talk about how to identify, build, and maintain boundaries in general. As you gain a better understanding of your own boundaries, and further develop this skill, you will begin to apply boundaries to different areas of your life.

1. **Identify Your Limits**

   The first step in setting boundaries is getting clear about what your limits are—emotional, mental, physical, spiritual, etc. You do this by paying increased attention to yourself and noticing what you can tolerate and accept as well as what makes you feel *uncomfortable* and *stressed*. These feelings will help you clarify your limits. It is important to remember that your limits are personal—your own—and therefore, they are likely to be different than the limits that others have (our friends, family members, colleagues etc.). Although challenging, it is most helpful if you do your best not to compare your limits with others' limits.

   What I may be willing or easily able to accept, may make *you* feel quite uncomfortable. This is then an important boundary for you. A recent example of bumping into a limit was a work opportunity that unexpectedly presented itself to me. I initially thought it would be an easy fit given my health expertise. However, I underestimated the effects of my personal history of loss, and how much this particular work setting would trigger these feelings. I knew immediately I had encountered a professional limit with the extremely strong feelings of discomfort that arose in me. I honored those feelings—my limit—and declined this work opportunity. Someone with a different personal history would most likely find this to be a wonderful professional opportunity.

The employer also respected my boundaries by not trying to persuade me to reconsider or to do it on a trial or part-time basis. Efforts to influence me to take the position, after I clearly stated I was very uncomfortable with the nature of the position, would have demonstrated a lack of consideration for my boundaries.

2. Pay Attention to Your Feelings

There are three key feelings that are often red flags or cues that you need to either set boundaries in a particular situation or that you are letting your boundaries slip (and not maintaining them). These feelings are (1) discomfort, (2) resentment, or (3) guilt. You can think of these feelings as cues to yourself that a boundary issue may be present. If a particular situation, person, or area of your life is leading you to feel uncomfortable, resentful, or guilty, and *it has happened several times,* this is an important cue.

For example, resentment often develops from feelings of being taken advantage of or not being appreciated. It's often a signal that you are extending yourself beyond your own limits because you feel guilty or want to be considered a good parent, spouse, sibling, child, friend, or employee. Another common contributor is someone else imposing their expectations, views, or values on you.

To determine how much attention the situation warrants and whether a boundary may need to be set, it is often helpful to think of these feelings on a continuum. For example, when a situation happens, ask yourself, "How uncomfortable, resentful, or guilty am I feeling now?" Rate your answer on a scale of 1–10 (10 highest). If your level of discomfort is a 3, you can consider this to be in the lower zone, having a mild affect on your emotions. Ratings of 4–6 are in the medium zone, indicating a more significant effect on you. Scores between 7 and 10 are considered in the high zone. As we discussed, boundaries are designed to protect you and your overall well-being. In this regard, consider setting a boundary if you are consistently rating a personal interaction or situation in the medium to high zone.

3. Give Yourself Permission to Set Boundaries

The biggest obstacles often experienced at some point, when considering setting a boundary, are the feelings of fear, guilt, and self-doubt—the anti-boundary musketeers—that show up. You might fear how the person will respond (e.g., angry, hurt) if you set and enforce your boundaries. You might feel guilty about speaking up or saying no to a family member or friend.

Often, people feel they should be able to cope with a situation and say yes, because that is what a good sibling, friend, or spouse would do. You may believe this despite the evidence that it is not good for you, leading you to feel drained and overextended at best, and taken advantage of at worst. You may question whether you even have the right or deserve to set boundaries in the first place. When these doubts occur, reaffirm to yourself that you do indeed have this right, so give yourself the permission to do so, and work to preserve them.

4. Consider Your Environment

When I was in training as a marriage and family therapist, one of the most valuable lessons I learned about human behavior was the incredible power of context.

The environment you are in, for example, serves as your context, and can have a strong influence on your behaviors, attitudes, and perceptions. Family and work environments are two examples of powerful contexts. Social circles are another. Why is it important to consider your environment when it comes to setting boundaries, you may be wondering? Your environment can either support your setting boundaries—making it easier for you—or present obstacles to boundary setting—making it more challenging for you. For example, consider your social circle of close friendships. Are these relationships generally reciprocal, with a natural give and take? Or do they feel lopsided, with you more often giving than receiving? If more lopsided, it will likely be more uncomfortable, and therefore more challenging, for you to begin to set boundaries or to maintain existing ones in these relationships.

Your work environment can also make it easier or more difficult for you to maintain your boundaries. For example, you might have a goal to have better work/life balance and plan to do this by leaving work no later than 5:30 p.m. daily. However, your coworkers typically work until 6:00 p.m. or 7:30 p.m. daily. As a result, there is an implicit expectation that you also work until at least 6:00 p.m. If you don't, you might be perceived as a slacker or seen as not a good, loyal employee. This office context thus makes it more challenging for you to honor your desired work/life boundary.

Setting Boundaries with Those Close to You

One common area where boundaries often need to be set is with well-meaning, caring, and often overly helpful family members and friends. At times, family members and friends can become overly involved in one's life—giving unsolicited advice and opinions, and outright telling you what to do. This often has the insidious effect of making you feel that you need their help and, more powerfully, making you feel that you can't do it yourself. How can you effectively address this?

Set boundaries by clearly communicating what you need and letting others know that although their intention to help is well-meaning, it would be more helpful to you if they would refrain from giving advice. You would like the time and mental space to work through this yourself, unless you directly ask them for advice or for their help.

You may feel uncomfortable bringing this up with family or friends for fear that they will be offended. But setting boundaries with those close to you can make your relationships stronger in the long run. Here are some ways to say this:

> "I love knowing that you want to be there for me, but I want to learn to problem-solve for myself. How about I ask you

when I would like your advice?

"When you think you have good advice to offer, I'd like you first to ask me, 'How can I help?' before you share your advice."

"It means a lot that you want to be there for me. I will do my best to let you know the type of support I need in the moment—for you to just listen; to problem-solve and explore options together; or to give me your advice."

For additional information on identifying and setting boundaries, see my article "10 Ways to Build and Preserve Better Boundaries" on Psych Central.

Potential Obstacles in Setting Boundaries

Fear of loss or threat to a relationship: Often, one of our greatest fears is that if we set boundaries, it might lead to the loss of an important relationship or threaten the status quo and lead to tension, hurt, or angry feelings. This fear can be enough for us to do nothing, despite our knowing better. We might deeply know it is in our best interest to establish limits, however, the fear can be paralyzing, especially if we have a history of loss in our past.

Fear of being called the "S" word: Many of us have a dread of being called S_____. Do you remember what that word is, which I discussed earlier in the chapter? Yes, that's right, SELFISH! The good news is that we are not alone. Upon being called selfish, we almost instinctually experience flickers of shame and even self-doubt. Are we being selfish, we might then ask ourselves. This shame or self-doubt can then lead us to question whether it's really necessary to set that limit after all. And the status quo remains. A wise, kind client of mine once said or borrowed, "If nothing changes, nothing changes."

Feelings of guilt: We also might experience significant guilt feelings when we imagine setting a limit with a family member, friend, or coworker. We don't want to hurt their feelings or embarrass them by setting a limit.

We might feel we should be able to handle the added demands on our time or energy. After all, isn't that what being a good partner or friend is about? Perhaps we feel guilty because we're not thinking so nicely toward Aunt Louise or coworker Susie. We feel increasing resentment or anger toward them and might feel guilty about having those negative emotions. Depending on our family background, personality, and relationship with this particular person, the degree of guilt can be very mild or quite extreme (9 or 10).

Any of the above fears or feelings, if strong enough, could become serious obstacles in our ability to either set an initial boundary or maintain it in the long term. If this is the case, and you know it is in your physical, emotional, spiritual, or financial best interest to set a boundary, then we strongly encourage you to seek professional support. Please contact a therapist or coach with a good knowledge of boundaries, and begin working together to overcome this challenge. The rewards (and support) you will receive are absolutely worth the effort, money, and courage involved. You can do it!

Moving Forward with Healthier Boundaries

What boundaries would be beneficial to set in order to establish and successfully maintain your new commitment to yourself?

What things would be helpful for you to begin doing (or stop doing) to be successful in setting those boundaries?

_____

_____

_____

_____

_____

FINDING TIME FOR HERSELF

Suzanne fantasizes daily about Calgon taking her away to the Caribbean for a few days of bed rest. She feels overwhelmed with the responsibilities of taking care of both her children and her aging parents. Her husband works nights, so he's less able to provide the emotional and physical support she needs. She frequently feels exhausted and now finds it difficult to resume her exercise routine. Her hair is turning gray, but she has no time to go to the hair stylist. The dog needs a grooming also, and imagine, he got an appointment before her! She hasn't had a physical in three years. No time. By the time she comes home, cooks, cleans up, packs lunches for her children and helps them with their homework, she has no time for herself, and it is usually past her desired bedtime. She is a teacher and increasingly finds herself taking work home to complete because of the increased demands. On the weekends, she visits her parents to do errands for them and to make some sense of their checkbook and bills.

SELF-CARE STRATEGIES

Suzanne would benefit from taking the self-care inventory to better assess her current level of stress. Since her self-care has decreased, she is either in the yellow or red zone. The inventory will help her assess this.

She could then identify what one or two boundaries would be helpful to set to free up some time for herself. For example, Suzanne could ask her children to help with the dishes after dinner and pack their own lunches. This would provide her with thirty to forty minutes per night for herself, which she could use toward her own self-care. A second boundary could be speaking with her siblings to better assist in her parent's caregiving.

BOUNDARIES AND TECHNOLOGY

We all know many people—and you very well might be one of them—who are married to their gadgets, whether it's their smartphone, iPad, laptop or some other tech toy.

All this accessibility and portability, while convenient and entertaining, has its downsides. It has created unrealistic expectations on the job (respond to email at nine o'clock p.m.? OK, boss!) and can hurt relationships, according to psychologist and coach Dana Gionta, Ph.D.

At her practice, she's seen how technology can compromise one's connection with loved ones. For instance, after work, some of her clients head straight to their computers. Instead of spending that time with loved ones, they inadvertently isolate and separate themselves, she said. Similarly, they may be physically present but not mentally or emotionally engaged. While they're sitting at the dinner table, they still might be glued to their gadgets, everyone's voices a mere hum in their head while they're dialed in.

As Gionta said, "One of the greatest gifts you can give to a loved one is your time and presence. But when we're attached to technology, we convey the message that our loved ones aren't important to us."

Gionta offered several suggestions for reeling in your gadget use and making sure that technology doesn't railroad your relationships or your life. At the core, it's about creating boundaries and sticking to them.

1. Talk to Your Family

   If you have a spouse and kids, have an open conversation with them about when it's appropriate to turn to technology and when it isn't. Think about your most important rituals and times of the day that you'd like to protect (like dinnertime or breakfast on the weekends) and those that are less important. During these less important lulls, everyone can take thirty minutes for tech time.

   However, Gionta underscored that every couple and family is different in what works for them. For instance, some couples prefer more alone time than others, so an hour of work or play at night on their laptops isn't a big deal. Other couples, however, use the evening as their sacred time. The important thing is to be on the same page and for everyone to feel respected and cared for.

2. Establish Structure

   If you have a demanding job or a hobby that requires being plugged in, establish a time every evening that you'll check your email and do your work. If you have kids, that time might be their bedtime.

Allotting the same time every night lets you accomplish your tasks without distraction, reduces your anxiety, and won't interfere with special moments, Gionta said. This way, you're fitting in technology when it works best for you—instead of doing everything around technology.

3. Maintain "Checks and Balances"

    Life is filled with exceptions, Gionta said. So there will be times when you'll have to take phone calls during dinner or work through the evening. The key, she said, is to check in with your loved ones to see if they feel like you're present and available.

4. Keep Gadgets in a Designated Spot

    Let's be honest, when your smartphone or iPad is close by, it's tempting to grab it and start surfing. Sometimes out of sight really is out of mind. By setting a specific place for using technology (like an office or den), you're creating a clear-cut physical boundary, she said.

5. Become More Self-Aware

    If you're constantly feeling the need to be productive, Gionta said to ask yourself, "Where is the pressure coming from?" Identify whether the driving force is external, like work, or internal, like your own need to be efficient. Once you're able to spot the source, you can take action to overcome it.

6. Get to the Root of the Problem

    Setting boundaries at home around tech use is valuable, but if the source of your stress is your job, you're just creating a band-aid. For instance, depending on your job, your boss may expect you to check email at 10 p.m. and respond immediately. Or there may be an implicit expectation at your office to work 24/7. If that's a problem for you, consider talking to your employer and setting realistic expectations.

If you're a small business owner, some of your clients may expect you to be at their beck and call early in the morning or late into the evening, especially if you're just starting out. Consider the pros and cons of being so accessible and speak up if that doesn't work for you.

7.   Notice When You're Slipping

How do you know when you're reverting to old habits? Think of your tech use like self-care, Gionta said. If you're spending less and less time each week being active or socializing with friends, you know your self-care is slipping. It might be subtle such as skipping your evening walk or talking to a close friend once a week instead of your usual two times.

In other words, watch for sly signs that your tech use is increasing. Maybe you're bringing your phone to the dinner table, using your laptop longer or your iPad before bed, or spending more time socializing on Facebook than with your family.

Remember that how often you use technology and let it blur the lines between work and life is up to you and your family. What matters is that you're running your gadgets—instead of them running you (Tartakovsky, 2011).

Chapter 15

Assertive Communication

*If you want to be happy, put your effort into
controlling the sail, not the wind.*

—Anonymous

"No, you may not borrow $1,000 and pay me back next week after you win the lotto!"

How many of us have a relative, friend, or coworker who has tried some version of this? ☺

Assertive communication is the ability to share our feelings, needs, limits, desires, values, and preferences, whether positive or negative, in an open, honest, and direct way. It is the number one skill in being able to set healthy boundaries. Although a very important first step, it is not enough to know our limits and needs. We then need to communicate this to whoever may be involved. Whether we're beginners at communicating assertively or more skilled at doing so, it may feel uncomfortable, and perhaps frightening at times, and more rarely, paralyzing to do so. This also depends on the *who*. We may find it easy to express our feelings, needs, or limits with some people, and extremely difficult to do so with others.

It does not mean we're weak or a failure if we find ourselves having great difficulty mustering up the courage to assertively communicate with a particular person. All bets are off, however, if this happens with everyone (only kidding!). This may mean that you have a more passive communication style that can be adapted over time, and with repeated practice, to a more assertive style. Remember to give yourself permission to make mistakes when practicing this skill. You may initially say something in a more aggressive or passive way until you begin to feel more comfortable and confident in communicating directly about something important to you, such as your needs, limits, or preferences.

So why is learning to communicate more assertively valuable and worth your investment of time and energy? Let's look at some of the key advantages of being able to assert your needs, feelings, wants, and limits. Another way of looking at this is to think of it also as the skill of standing up for your Self.

Key Advantages of Assertive Communication

It helps us get our needs and wants met and gives others the opportunity to assist us in these efforts.

It leads us to feeling more confident and proud of ourselves (empowering feelings).

It provides us with a greater sense of control in our lives and reduces unnecessary anxiety in the process.

It allows people to know where they stand with us, creating greater honesty, respect, and trust in our relationships.

It builds stronger, healthier relationships by addressing issues as they come up and not letting emotions build up and ultimately erupt like a volcano.

It protects us from being controlled and/or taken advantage of by others.

It allows us to more closely live what is true for us by more freely making choices that support who we are and what we want for our lives.

Tips to Communicating More Assertively

Use "I" Statements

"*I* don't feel comfortable with you borrowing my favorite dress."

"*I* don't like it when you make negative comments about my driving (or tell me how to drive)."

"*I* would like you to stop doing that (specific behavior)."

"Next time, *I* would appreciate it if you would call first before dropping by."

Use "When, I" Strategy

"*When* you borrow my things without asking, *I* feel like you don't respect me."

"*When* you drop by the house unexpectedly, *I* feel uncomfortable because it interrupts what I'm doing."

If the behavior(s) in question continue despite assertively addressing it with the person, then it is time to add a consequence to the behavior.

Use Consequences

"If you do this again, I am going to . . . "

Key Tips When Stating Consequences

The simpler and shorter the consequence is stated, the clearer and more powerful it is. As best you can, speak in a manner that is more matter of fact, with a moderate tone. If you yell it, however tempting, it significantly dilutes its power to influence.

Identify a consequence you know will have some effect on the individual. The key is moderation. You do not want a consequence that has such a little effect (i.e., give me a quarter every time you make a negative comment about my driving) or too much, which will appear outlandish and unrealistic (give me $50 for each negative comment). You will not be taken seriously.

Be mindful to make the consequence match the crime, I (Dana) mean the behavior. Be careful not to make the consequence harsh. This will lead to resentment and adversely affect the quality of the relationship. Think about how you would feel if someone gave you the same consequence based on the behavior. Does it seem reasonable and fair, with moderate effect? If you are not sure, ask a trusted friend, family member, or coworker their thoughts about the consequence.

Giving a consequence might eventually become setting a boundary with the person if the behavior in question continues, despite several consequences given. For example, you've given several consequences to a person about making negative comments about your driving, yet despite this, the person continues the behavior. It is now time to set a boundary to protect yourself, especially your self-esteem and self-confidence. An example of setting a boundary in this situation would be to tell this person that the next time he makes a negative comment, you will discontinue driving with him, or that in the future you will take separate cars, or he will need to find someone else to give him a ride. After a period of time, you can revisit his ability to drive with you and respect your boundary.

A good way to think about the difference between a consequence and a boundary is that a consequence generally has to do with the other person. The consequence is directed at this person and involves something he/she needs to do or not do (i.e., give me $10 for every time you swear; no phone for one week). A boundary has to do with you—protecting or honoring yourself. You are the one taking the action (i.e., not driving with this person; attending your favorite class despite disapproval by others; answering the phone only between the designated hours you gave).

Here is an easy way to remember this:

assertively communicating + a behavioral action <u>you</u> take = setting a boundary

Each of these involves a skill, so seek support if needed, and give yourself permission to *do it messy*. There are no mistakes when learning and practicing something new—only learning efforts along the learning curve!

Chapter 16

Quality of Our Relationships

Simple kindness to one's Self and all that lives is the most powerful transformational force of all.

—David Hawkins

Our relationships can have a huge impact on the quality of our emotional and physical health and on our overall life satisfaction. Being surrounded by family, friends, and neighbors who love and support us and make us feel cared for and respected, enhances our sense of ourselves. They encourage us, inspire us, listen to us, respect us in both words and actions—always actions—and consider our feelings. There is a natural reciprocity in positive relationships, an easy balance between giving and taking, which leads to our feeling valued and appreciated. We feel at peace when we're around them, we can be our true selves, and we feel safe—emotionally, mentally, physically, and spiritually. Such relationships often bring out our better selves. In essence, positive, supportive relationships = good self-care.

Unhealthy, negative relationships are those that often make us feel bad about ourselves or parts of ourselves. They also often make us feel insecure, fearful, and less than: less competent, less intelligent, less attractive, less liked. There are often negative comments, criticisms, judgments, blame, shoulds, the right/wrong way of talk as well as domineering, emotionally manipulative behaviors that lead to one feeling wrong, guilty, not good enough, and drained. Over time, such relationships enact a huge cost in terms of our stress level, our ability to maintain good self-care practices, our emotional health, our esteem, and eventually our physical health. These relationships may become toxic to our health and well-being if they continue over the long term. In regard to self-care, these relationships may make it very difficult for us to either begin or maintain good self-care practices because we often feel very drained from the stress, conflict, and roller-coaster nature of this type of relationship.

If you believe there is an individual in your inner circle—those closest to you—who frequently makes you feel this way about yourself, then we strongly recommend that you seek professional support to more effectively address this matter.

Evaluating the Quality of Relationships

Self-care is also about periodically evaluating the quality of the relationships in our lives. This includes our relationships with our spouses or partners, parents, children, in-laws, close friends, and coworkers.

How would you describe these relationships? Supportive, nurturing, loving, caring, attentive, respectful, fun? Or stressful, conflictual, draining, uncomfortable, anxiety-provoking, unpredictable? The answers to these questions, for each close relationship you have, will give you a better understanding of the overall quality of each relationship. This information will help you determine how specific relationships might be impacting your self-care and the quality of your life in general.

Relationships that we feel are supportive, caring, positive, and healthy serve to enhance our life and well-being. They generally lift our mood, energy level, motivation, and overall outlook on life. All of these wonderful benefits from such positive, supportive relationships often then make it easier for us to care for our Selves and to regularly practice good self-care.

When you have one or more relationships in your life that either drain you, make you feel less than or bad about yourself, lead you to feeling less hopeful or positive about the world or your future in general, it is likely that your emotional well-being and self-care is being negatively affected. It doesn't matter how confident, strong, and resilient you truly are. You may tell yourself that you can handle or cope with such behavior. The reality is that if you are exposed to these kinds of relationships on a regular basis, over an extended period of time, it is very likely that these relationships will eventually wear you down, emotionally, physically, and spiritually. They will compromise the quality of your life and those closest to you because you are not able to bring your happier, energetic, loving, and present Self to those healthier relationships.

Ask Yourself How You Feel

What if it's not so clear if a relationship is healthy or good for you? Years ago I came across a simple but powerful question that I (Dana) and my clients have found very helpful in getting clarity about the quality of a particular relationship. Ask yourself:

> Do I feel better or worse after spending time or interactng with this person?

Consider asking yourself this question multiple times and keeping track of your responses. You will eventually gain clarity.

Ask How Your Body Feels

Another cue to how a person or situation makes you feel is to pay attention to your body. Ask yourself how your body feels:

> Does my body feel more or less energized after speaking with this person?

What happens to your energize-o-meter after spending time with this person? Does it generally go up or down? These are additional cues which might help you better understand why you feel drained by some relationships and energized and lightened by others.

Gaining Clarity

Consider setting boundaries within the relationship. For example, limit your time spent with this person or identify the topics you will and won't talk about. If necessary, you may need to discontinue the relationship altogether if you believe the cost to your well-being and happiness is too high.

If you find yourself needing to do these exercises with the same person multiple times, it is likely this relationship is truly not in your best interest. Remember, this is a process that takes skill and time to gain clarity and take action, so be gentle with yourself and give yourself permission to make mistakes. Mistakes are opportunities to learn about yourself, so be gentle and commit to learning the lessons and falling forward toward a more peaceful, happier you.

MOVING ON

Paul relocated out west nine months ago and really loves it there. He's made some good friends and enjoys his new job and colleagues. He misses his family and friends; however, he knows he made the right decision. Paul notices lately that every time he speaks with his long-time friend back home, he feels put down and judged. He doesn't understand what's happening and wonders why his friend is acting this way. He feels sad and confused about the change in the friendship.

SELF-CARE STRATEGIES

Paul acknowledges that this friendship is now negatively affecting his feelings about himself. He considers speaking with his good friend about his observations and the effects on him.

Paul could inquire about possible factors contributing to his friend's behavior so he can have a better understanding.

If future conversations continue to be hurtful to Paul, he intends to assertively request the behavior change he needs from his friend, and possibly limit their frequency of communication until the situation improves.

Chapter 17

Obstacles to Good Self-Care

Mistakes are always forgivable, if one has the courage to admit them.

—Bruce Lee

Most of us have very good intentions of engaging in a self-care routine consistently. We know it is good for us, that we would feel better if we did, and that our family and friends would like us to do so. However, one of the main reasons we often don't practice regular self-care is because of one of the obstacles listed below.

The #1 Mistake

Many times, we tell ourselves *we don't have time* to fit in our self-care practices this week because we're extra busy or we're too tired given the increased demands. This is the # 1 mistake we all often make, including myself, at times. It is when the demands begin to increase that we need to hold on tight to our regular practices and maintain good self-care. This is especially true when we are expecting the busyness to last more than one to two weeks. This sounds counter-intuitive, I know. However, by maintaining and even increasing our self-care behaviors during these times, we can have increased energy and concentration and will be in a better frame of mind to accomplish whatever tasks we have.

The #2 Mistake

After sharing the #1 mistake the majority of us make, can you guess what the #2 mistake is that most often sabotages our self-care practices? Yes?
The #2 mistake is the belief that it is selfish and self-indulgent to

practice good self-care, and therefore, that we are selfish or indulgent if we do so. It is perceived as too much time spent on ourselves, which is taking time away from loved ones and others. It is also often misperceived as thinking very highly of ourselves (who do you think you are) and, as a result, not being considerate of the needs of others. Both of these perceptions could not be further from the truth. It is only when we take good care of our emotional and physical well-being that we can truly be there, be present, with others in a positive way. This is similar to the preflight safety instruction to put on our own oxygen masks before assisting our children or others around us. Why is this so important? Because it is only by first taking care of ourselves that we can ensure we will be in the mental and physical condition to meet the needs of our children or companions. This applies to our personal and professional lives as well.

Temperament and Family Roles

Caregiving Nature/Role of Caregiver in Childhood

If we have a very caring or giving nature or grew up in a family where we were the appointed caregiver, it might be more challenging for us to engage in good self-care. There are several reasons for this. First, we generally think of the needs and concerns of others, before our own needs. Second, it may feel very uncomfortable to focus on and deliberately take time for ourselves, so it is easier to avoid it and the unpleasant feelings. When something is unfamiliar to us, it can initially feel quite uncomfortable until we give ourselves permission and build a new habit. Third, as a caregiver, the thought of someone perceiving us as selfish might be very disturbing to our sense of self, and therefore, we avoid this risk. This is understandable. However, in the long run, it is not healthy and not in our best interest or our inner circle's best interest. The good news is that it is possible to find balance in our caregiving tendency by making time for ourselves and establishing a healthier give and take. Again, it is not selfish, but self-consideration. We can give ourselves a gift by giving ourselves permission. This is an invaluable first step in better self-care.

Overly Responsible Tendency: Taking on Responsibility for Me, You, and the Dog

Some of us, by nature or nurture, grow up to be very responsible adults. If this is the case, we may have a tendency to take on not only what is our responsibility, but also what is our loved ones' or peers' responsibilities. This often results in what we call over-functioning behavior on our part, and under-functioning or "slacking" on their part. If we believe that others wouldn't do it as well as we would do it or as quickly as we do, or if we believe that others just wouldn't do it at all, then we often jump in and get it done ourselves. At least we know it will be done and done right! The problem with this is that it takes time and physical as well as emotional energy to do others' work for them. This leaves less time and energy (our personal resources) to rejuvenate and do more of what *we* really want (i.e., take a class, be with friends and family, enjoy a hobby) or just relax. Over time, this can lead to resentful feelings or resignation that others always come first, and feelings that we're really not as important as others. In this regard, we are teaching people how to treat and interact with us. If others know we will do it, then their own motivation and sense of responsibility often declines.

Our tendency to be over-responsible may also show up emotionally, not just through our behaviors and what we *do* for others. We may take responsibility for others' feelings, and feel guilty or bad about ourselves as a result. For example, if our child or spouse feels hurt or angry in response to something we did (i.e., set a boundary) or said, we are not necessarily *the cause* of their feelings. It is important to take a moment to consider whether we do have some responsibility or whether it is another's personal issue and something that person needs to take responsibility for.

We Like Being Needed

Many of us like being needed. It gives us a sense of importance and often provides us with a sense of meaning and purpose in life. This can be a driving factor in what leads us to continually help others or overextend ourselves for family or friends at home, or for our boss or coworkers. It is also a way to enhance our self-esteem, as we notice others coming to us for assistance or help. This tendency can be very appealing and feel quite good, at times. It can serve us well and not necessarily be a problem for us. However, it can come with costs that in the long run may be quite high. This is something we need to evaluate. For example, sometimes as a result of being overextended, we don't have enough time to exercise two to three times a week or make time for our favorite hobbies as often because of this.

BALANCING HARD WORK AND HAPPINESS

Jerry is a hardworking securities broker at a well-known financial institution. He has been with this company for ten years. It is not uncommon for him to enter work at 7:00 a.m. and leave somewhere between 8:00 and 9:00 p.m. One day, after having a particularly stressful week, his boss told him that he was being promoted, which meant increased pay and increased responsibility, including working some weekends. Jerry doesn't mind hard work. In fact, his diligence and industriousness has always been praised and rewarded. When he heard the news of his promotion, however, he couldn't help but feel disheartened and filled with dread. Initially, he could not understand why he was not feeling more elated and optimistic, after all, his competence was being recognized for a promotion, and he would be receiving more pay. But Jerry also noticed he was more prone to irritability lately and seemed to have a short fuse. His wife and children had commented that he seemed not to laugh much anymore. Could it be that Jerry's devotion to working so much, over such a long period of time, has impacted his mood and relationships with others?

SELF-CARE STRATEGIES

Jerry is now more tuned in to his feelings. He recognizes that he is not feeling comfortable or excited about this promotion. He takes time to reflect and identifies that the promotion would compromise the little work/life balance he already has.

Jerry could explore his options with a trusted friend, colleague, or family member. He considers the costs/benefits of accepting the promotion and the importance of having a conversation with his boss around the demands and expected schedule for the new position. This way he can make an informed decision. He realizes that increased financial well-being cannot come at the expense of his personal or family's well-being and happiness any longer.

Chapter 18

Putting Self-Care into Practice in Your Life

What saves a man is to take a step. Then another step.

—C. S. Lewis

You are almost at the end of our book. Many of you are already practicing self-care at least some of the time, and some of you are living it on a daily basis. For others, it has become a way of life for you. Every one of you, congratulate yourselves! Whatever you have been able to do up to this point is a success. Especially since, as you have just learned, obstacles often exist that compromise your ability to make changes in your life, despite your best intentions.

The Blindness Factor

A key observation I (Dana) have made over the past fifteen years working with numerous clients and in my personal life and lives of family members and friends is what I like to call our blindness factor. We are often blind to our own changes! Many of us have difficulty recognizing the changes we are making (or have made), similar to our difficulty in recognizing our strengths. We often feel we are not making progress or haven't grown as much as we truly have.

The truth is that most change occurs incrementally, in small steps, which over time lead to significant and powerful changes. Because of this, we often don't recognize how we are changing and moving successfully toward the person we wish to become, or the life and goals we want. This is especially true if we have setbacks along the way. We either don't anticipate them, or we think of setbacks as signs of failure.

This cannot be further from the truth. Setbacks are an inherent part of change, any change.

What is most important to remember and do is to continue to give yourself credit for each step you take and believe in your ability to change. If you truly want what you say is important to you, you will eventually reach your goal. Build on your strengths and focus on your victory steps toward what you want. If you need extra support along the way, be courageous and ask for it. You are more resourceful, deserving, and capable than you might know! You have more options and possibilities for your Self and your life than you can imagine.

The BEFORE You

Before reading this book, you may have been experiencing something very similar to the real-life examples listed below. Let's take a look:

> You have several people in your life who you often socialize with who complain and drain your energy.

> You frequently return home from work feeling stressed and overwhelmed.

> When someone says or does something that hurts you or makes you feel bad about yourself, you say nothing or try to ignore it.

> You feel torn in many directions with everyone wanting something from you, and no time for yourself.

> You have wanted to make a major change in your life (e.g. go back to school) for several years, but your parents and your partner disapprove. You feel selfish and guilty, so you decide not to make any changes.

> By the time you've helped the kids with homework, finished household chores, and talked on the phone, it is 11:00 p.m. You feel frustrated and upset because you promised yourself you would start getting to bed earlier.

You are feeling stressed and decide you need a vacation. You schedule a break that works well for you and the company. While on vacation, you feel you should check in with the office and review your emails. There is an email from your boss requesting immediate information regarding a project. A wave of anxiety comes over you.

You discover your co-worker has been gossiping about you. You feel hurt and betrayed since you thought this person was also a friend. You are afraid if you try to speak with the co-worker about it, you will get so angry that you will either explode or cry.

After much apprehension, you decide to go on a date at a restaurant with someone you've been talking with on the phone. Within the first hour, you feel very uncomfortable with this person's behavior. You want to leave but don't want to be rude. You feel trapped.

The AFTER You

Now that you've read this book, you may already be experiencing something very similar to the real-life examples listed below. Let's take a look:

You made the decision to surround yourself with more positive, energizing people. You now set limits with anyone who complains or drains your energy by limiting the time you spend with them (e.g. seeing/speaking with them less often, or discontinuing the relationship if necessary).

You now come home feeling more energized, after starting to take brief meditation/rejuvenation breaks at work. You are mindful to periodically assess your stress (e.g. green, yellow or red zone) by reviewing any changes to your regular self-care routine.

You recognize and honor your feelings more. Now, you typically let others know when they have hurt you and what you would like them to do differently in the future. You are able to set a boundary when needed.

You make yourself more of a priority, with regular time for yourself each day. You have learned that to be there for others, you first need to be there for your Self.

You recognize that your needs and desires are important, and that pursuing them will make you happier and more fulfilled. You give yourself permission to do what is best for You, despite others' disapproval.

You set boundaries with family members and friends to honor your bedtime schedule. Extenuating circumstances may arise, however you are regularly getting seven to eight hours of sleep.

You are committed to work/life balance and know that a key purpose of a vacation is to rejuvenate yourself. You have a discussion with your boss about the amount of communication, if any, would be expected, while you are away.

After developing your assertive communication skills, you are better able to speak with your colleague about his/her hurtful statements. You allow yourself time to process your feelings, and when calmer, you assertively express your feelings about the situation and the behavior change you desire.

You tune in more to both your feelings and body signals. You honor your discomfort with others' behaviors, and you share your feelings and set boundaries. If your feelings are not honored, you are now prepared to leave uncomfortable situations.

Before and After Reflection Exercise

Considering the above before and after examples, take a moment to reflect on the subtle, incremental changes you likely have already made.

List one or two of these small but significant changes.

Incremental steps I have taken:

_____

_____

_____

_____

One of the most powerful practices we use with clients is to help them identify the positive, courageous changes they have made within the past three, six, nine, or twelve months. What they could not do three months ago, they are now doing! They are changing, growing and becoming a stronger, healthier, happier version of themselves, step by step.

An empowering way to remember the incremental changes you make is to keep what I like to call a "victory list." You may call it anything you like. Consider starting one after completing this book.

The final lessons in this book are especially exciting because they are about the creative and personal ways you can bring together the stress management and self-care practices you have learned throughout this book into your daily life, and why it is important to do both.

Chapter 19

Integrating Stress Management and Self-Care: A Closer Look

The purpose of life, after all, is to live it, to taste experience to the utmost, to reach out eagerly and without fear for newer and richer experience.

—Eleanor Roosevelt

After reading this book, you now have a good foundation of the key principles and practices of both stress management and self-care. Although we divided the book into separate sections for each, both are integrally connected and are best practiced together in our daily lives. Why is that you may ask? Below we will provide an overview for both stress management and self-care and explore what is the important relationship between them.

The Stress Management and Self-Care Relationship

What is the relationship between stress management and self-care? We believe the relationship between stress management and self-care is a bidirectional one, as seen in Figure 8.

FIGURE 8. STRESS MANAGEMENT AND SELF-CARE RELATIONSHIP.

| Stress Management | ⟷ | Self-Care |

You may notice now that when you think about stress management or self-care, there is a natural tendency to consider the other. For instance, if your stress is increasing and beginning to have a negative impact on your physical or emotional health, then you will want to evaluate your present level of self-care. On the other hand, if your self-care practices have diminished, then you are at risk for greater stress. You have likely slipped into the yellow zone, indicating that it is time to boost both your self-care and stress-management practices.

A good stress management practice is an act of self-care, and healthy levels of self-care act as protection against the negative effects of stress. For example, taking care of your nutrition, exercise, and boundary setting minimizes current stress and can serve to inoculate you against future stress. When you address your stress directly (through one or more of the practices that are offered in this book), you enable your body and mind to be more present, which improves your focus and energy, allowing you to practice better self-care. Each of these areas of practice powerfully influences the other. Stress management and self-care go hand and hand in improving your overall quality of life.

Personal Stress Management +
Self-Care Integration

Take a moment to consider the top three discoveries you made about yourself after reading this book.

My top three self-discoveries:

1. _____

2. _____

3. _____

You can refer back to your three top discoveries when creating your individual action plan (Appendix B) later in the book.

POSITIVE MOMENTUM

Jenette became aware that her stress level had gone up over the past two months. After thinking about it, she realized she was feeling more uncertainty at work due to organizational changes but also more uncertainty internally as she started to daydream about a career change. Finances were also a worry as she hadn't gotten a raise in several years, and she felt increased worry about general cost-of-living increases in providing for her family. She noticed feeling a bit anxious and more distracted, not able to be as present or enjoy her time with her family. She also started to feel bad about herself. She felt she wasn't as successful as she thought she should be by now. Jenette also realized that she hadn't exercised in three weeks and had cancelled on plans with friends twice in the past month.

She decided to share some of her worries with a good friend. She knew the emotional support would help. Her friend could problem solve strategies with her to assist her in taking a more proactive approach. She also decided to get up fifteen minutes earlier than usual and either meditate, journal, or reflect on her spiritual readings as a way of more calmly starting her day. At night, she began walking after dinner to give herself some alone time to reflect and explore her options. She knew the exercise would help her feel better.

She began exploring her desire for a career change, to do something more creative. At first, she had negative thoughts about what others would think, that she was being irresponsible in considering leaving a secure job, and feared that she didn't have sufficient experience to change careers. Jenette recognized that she was thinking negatively and began practicing thought-stopping around career-related fears. She also recognized she needed to set a boundary with her parents and discontinue discussing her career concerns with them at this time. It just made them anxious, and she would then often feel more fearful afterwards. A coworker suggested she speak to a career coach to help her identify her natural strengths, unique abilities, and passions. She thought that might help, so she scheduled an appointment to meet with someone who came highly recommended.

Over time, she noticed feeling less stressed and a bit more energized and hopeful about her future. She began to really look forward to her mornings meditating and reading, as well as looking forward to her evening walks by herself. She enjoyed her time with her family and friends more now, and noticed that she was laughing more. Others began commenting that she seemed calmer and was smiling more often. Jenette realized change takes time and began to feel more confident that the steps and direction she was taking for herself and her family were positive ones. She felt proud of herself.

My Key Takeaways

Now that you have considered three important discoveries about yourself with regard to stress management and self-care and have read a vignette on how to integrate both, we would also like you to think about some tips, strategies, and general knowledge that you have learned from this book that you would like to remember and potentially share with others (i.e., children, family, coworkers).

The key items I have learned and intend to use in my stress management and self-care practice:

1. _____

2. _____

3. _____

4. _____

5. _____

Managing stress well and incorporating good self-care practices are essential to creating a psychology of health and well-being, and we hope by now you have an effective road map to help you get there. By using the principles, practices, and exercises of this book, we believe that you will be able to improve your health, well-being, and overall quality of life.

APPENDIX A:

Our Approach to Stress Management and Self-Care

What We Practice for Our Own Good Stress Management and Self-Care

Dan's Practice

I balance a busy work schedule with social events and time spent with friends and family. Especially as an extrovert, I have a high need for spending time with a lot of people.

Spending time in regular prayer.

I exercise regularly (three to four times per week).

I plan enough time for a relaxing vacation, which for me usually involves mountains.

I spend time doing creative activities that I enjoy, like improvisational acting and vocal training.

If my boundaries have been violated in some way, either by someone asking too much of me, treating me poorly, or verbally stepping over the line, it usually registers in my body as an uncomfortable feeling or sensation. My task is to listen to this and take action to establish appropriate boundaries right away.

I tune into my body when eating and ask, "Am I full? What does my body need right now?"

The answer to the question, "Could I drink more water today?" is almost always yes.

I take unusual opportunities to cultivate mindful awareness (i.e., on the subway, on line at the bank, in a formal setting)

I spend fifteen purposeful minutes *not* looking at my smartphone!

Never underestimate a good opportunity to shut up sometimes! (I engage in quiet reflection, which is a great skill to develop for managing stress and practicing self-care).

Dana's Practice

I make doing something fun each week a priority (i.e., watch a funny movie/sitcom; take a dance class; go ice skating)

I get together with family or friends weekly to have some enjoyable and relaxing social time.

I stretch every morning for ten to fifteen minutes daily. I have been doing this for the past twenty years, since having previous back issues. I do it as a preventive measure, which has been very effective.

I exercise three to four times per week. I also do something physically active each season (i.e., biking in the spring, swimming in the summer, skiing in the winter).

I nurture my love of learning in some way, such as by learning a new skill or taking a course that interests me. (I recently took a hospitality course, given my passion for travel.)

I listen to my intuition regarding whether a person,

situation, or environment is good for me or not.

I consider what boundary I need to set, and then I act on that decision.

When I begin to feel a need to recharge emotionally or physically (after assessing my stress zone), I schedule a massage, an overnight weekend retreat, or another relaxing experience, if possible.

I take a vacation every year, during which I set clear boundaries around work and technology. This allows me to feel renewed and gain a fresh perspective.

I spend time in nature and slow everything down (speed of walking, talking, and breathing), which signals my body to slow down and rest.

Our Quick Stress-Reducing/Self-Care Tips

- Press the pause button. Intentionally slow down your movements, your pace of walking and talking.

- Identify and replace negative, stress-inducing thoughts with positive, realistic ones.

- Take deep breaths in through your nose and out through your mouth. Let your stomach rise and fall easily (I know, your pants/skirt are too tight for that!)

- Take a five-to-ten-minute walk, in nature if possible. If not, walk in any environment that is calming.

- Think of all the people in your life who love and care about you.

APPENDIX B:

Your Individual Action Plan

We would like to partner with you in helping you achieve success based on integrating the information that you have learned in this book. By developing your own individual action plan and monitoring it regularly, you can have greater success in achieving your goals..

What is an Individual Action Plan?

The Individual Action Plan is not to be used as a way to beat yourself up, to prove to yourself how you are unable to make progress, or to put unhealthy stress on yourself. To the contrary, it is your personal story, condensed into a self-accountable plan that can be monitored and adjusted so that you can improve and achieve the success you have dreamed of achieving!

Stress Management and Self-Care Reflection

First let's look at what you are currently doing to manage stress and to practice good self-care. Consider asking family and friends for their feedback and observations about you in this area.

My current stress management practices:

1. _____

2. _____

3. _____

My current self-care practices:

1. _____

2. _____

3. _____

Stress Management and Self-Care Goals

Think about what your goals are for stress management and self-care. What are the top three goals you would like to work on after reading this book?

My top three personal overall goals for stress management and self-care:

1. _____

2. _____

3. _____

Stress Management and Self-Care Action Steps

Action steps will help you go from thinking about goals to beginning the journey toward realizing them. We have listed some examples of actions steps below and some space for you to consider and write down your own.

Example action steps for stress management:

- Practice a breathing exercise of my choice from this book.

- Write down negative, catastrophic thoughts and replace them with positive, realistic ones.

Stress management action steps I agree to take to achieve my goals:

_____

_____

_____

Example action steps for self-care:

- Identify one area where you would like to set a boundary.

- Review your self-care inventory and identify one item you would like to begin working on.

Self-care action steps I agree to take to achieve my goals

_____

_____

_____

Potential Obstacles to Taking Action Toward Your Goals

Consider your goals and the action steps that you listed above. What may be some potential obstacles that you may encounter?

Examples of obstacles to achieving these action steps:

- Fatigue.

- Negative self-speak and sabotaging thoughts that convince me that practice will not make a difference.

- Choosing an old, unhealthy way of coping (i.e., smoking, drinking alcohol, watching television, spending time with people who drain us)

Potential obstacles that may limit my action steps:

_____

_____

_____

Pro-Active Mental Tools You Can Use to Help Achieve Your Goals

We have listed a few reminders of tools that you can use to begin the process of achieving your goals. Feel free to use these, review some additional tools found in previous chapters, or come up with some on your own!

If you are tired, say to yourself:

"Even when I am feeling tired, I know after this brief practice that I am likely to feel more energized and relaxed. A little goes a long way!"

Replace negative thoughts with more realistic, positive ones:

"Doing these practices will make a difference. They will make me feel better, develop resistance to future stressors, and change the pattern of my behaviors that are no longer working for me."

The journey of 1000 miles begins with a single step. Say to yourself:

"For this moment, I will make a different choice. I am going to do ten to fifteen minutes of exercise (or mindfulness meditation, or prayer, or other form of reflection)."

Time Line for Integrating Practices

Having a time line can help you take important, incremental steps toward your goals. Again, we advise against using the time line as a rigid structure that increases stress or feelings of inadequacy. Use it as a flexible tool that can help you integrate the practices over time in a way that better serves you and your quality of life. Review the goals that you wrote down at the beginning of this chapter and decide on when and how you would like to integrate the tools and practices into your time line below.

Personal Goal #1: _____

Desired date of integration of tools and practices:

_____

How will you evaluate your progress?

_____

_____

_____

_____

_____

Personal Goal #2: _____

Desired date of integration of tools and practices:

_____

How will you evaluate your progress?

_____

_____

_____

_____

_____

Personal Goal #3: _____

Desired date of integration of tools and practices:

_____

How will you evaluate your progress?

_____

_____

_____

_____

_____

REFERENCES

Anjali, Gurani. *Ways of Yoga*. Amityville, NY. Vajra Press, 1993.

American Psychological Association. (2013). *Stress in America: Missing the Health Care Connection*. Retrieved from http://www.apa.org/news/press/releases/stress/2012/full-report.pdf

American Psychological Association. (2013a). *Communication Technology: Implications for Work and Well-Being*. Retrieved from http://www.apaexcellence.org/assets/general/2013-work-and-communication- technology-survey-final.pdf

American Psychological Association. (2013b). *2013 Work and Well-Being Survey*. Retrieved from http://www.apaexcellence.org/assets/general/2013-work-and-wellbeing- survey-results.pdf

American Psychological Association. (2012). *Workforce Retention Survey*. Retrieved from http://www.apaexcellence.org/assets/general/2012-retention-survey-final.pdf

American Psychological Association. (2009). *Stress in America 2009*. Retrieved from http://www.apa.org/news/press/releases/stress-exec-summary.pdf

American Psychological Association (2004). *Employer Recommendations. Public Policy, Work, and Families: The Report of the APA Presidential Initiative on Work and Families*. Retrieved from http://www.apa.org/work-family/employers.html

Blessing, B. & Gibbins, I. "Autonomic Nervous System, Fig.1"

Scholarpedia 3(7) (2008): 2787.

Mann, Denise (2013) (reviewed by Laura J. Martin, M.D.). Alcohol and a Good Night's Sleep Don't Mix. Retrieved from http://www.webmd.com/sleep-disorders/news/20130118/alcohol-sleep

Bureau of Labor Statistics. (2001). [Table R67] *Number and percent distribution of nonfatal occupational injuries and illnesses involving days away from work by nature of injury or illness and number of days away from work*. Retrieved from http://www.bls.gov/iif/oshwc/osh/case/ostb1222.pdf

Cannon, W.B. (1929). *Bodily Changes in Pain, Hunger, Fear, and Rage*. New York and London. D. Appelton and Company, 1915.

Frone, M. R., Russell, M., & Barnes, G. M. Work-Family Conflict, Gender and Health Related Outcomes: A study of employed parents in two community samples. *Journal of Occupational Health Psychology, 1,* (1996): 57-69.

Holmes, T. H. & Rahe R. H. The Social Readjustment Rating Scale. *Journal of Psychosomatic Research,* Volume 11, Issue 2, (1967).

Kabat-Zinn, Jon. *Wherever You Go, There You Are: Mindfulness meditation in every-day life.* New York, NY. Hyperion, 1994.

Kabat-Zinn, Jon. *Full Catastrophe Living: Using the wisdom of your body and mind to face stress, pain, and illness.* McHenry, IL. Delta Publishing Company, 1990.

Lehrer, P., Woolfolk, R. L. & Sime W. E. *Principles and Practice of Stress Management,* New York, NY. Guilford Press, 1993.

Davis, M., Eshelman, E. R., & McKay, M. *The Relaxation and Stress Reduction Workbook,* 6th Ed. Oakland, CA. New Harbinger Publications, 2008.

Neal, M. N. & Hammer, L. B. *Working Couples Caring for Children and Aging Parents: Effects on work-family fit, well-being, and work (a longitudinal study funded by the Alfred P. Sloan Foundation).* Mahwah, NJ. Lawrence Erlbaum Associates, 2007.

Priest, Simon. *The Adventure Experience Paradigm.* In J.C. Miles, & S. Priest (Eds.), Adventure Recreation. State College PA: Venture Publishing, 1990.

PubMed Health: Informed Health Online. Institute for Quality and Efficiency in Health Care (IQWiG) What Is Burnout Syndrome? Retrieved from http://www.ncbi.nlm.nih.gov/pubmedhealth/PMH0050545/

Rosch, P. J. *The Quandary of Job Stress Compensation.* Health and Stress, Volume 3, 1-4 (2001).

Sagawa Y., Kondo H., Matsubuchi N., et. al. Alcohol Has a Dose-Related Effect on Parasympathetic Nerve Activity During Sleep, Alcoholism: *Clinical and Experimental Research,* Volume 35, Issue 11 (2011).

Shaar, M. & Britton, K. *Smarts and Stamina: The busy person's guide to optimal health and performance.* New York, NY. Positive Psychology Press, 2011.

Tan, Chade-Meng. *Search Inside Yourself: The Unexpected Path to Achieving Success, Happiness (and World Peace).* New York, NY. Harper Collins, 2012.

Tartakovsky, Margarita. (2011). Is Technology Running Your Life? Set Some

Boundaries. Retrieved from *PsychCentral*.com http://psychcentral.com/lib/is-technology-running-your-life-set-some-boundaries/0008730

Tartakovsky, Margarita. (2011). 10 Ways to Build and Preserve Better Boundaries. *Psych Central.* Retrieved on October 23, 2014, from http://psychcentral.com/lib/10-way-to-build-and-preserve-better-boundaries/0007498

Yerkes R. M. & Dodson J. D. *The Relation of Strength of Stimulus to Rapidity of Habit-Formation.* Journal of Comparative Neurology and Psychology Volume 18, 459–482 (1908).

TO OUR READERS,

With much gratitude and appreciation, we wish you success on your journey (and individual action plan) toward greater stress management and self-care! We would love to hear your stories, lessons learned, successes, and the strategies you found most helpful along the way. We also welcome any questions you may have or feedback that you would like to give us. Get in touch with us at: fromstressedtocentered@gmail.com.

If you enjoyed our book and found it helpful, we would be grateful if you would share it with your family, friends, and co-workers. We would also appreciate it if you took some time to review our book on amazon.com and share what specific things you liked about it. Many thanks! The better we collectively learn to manage our stress and take care of our Selves, the healthier and happier we ultimately all will be!

—Dana & Dan

REFERENCES

Anjali, Gurani. *Ways of Yoga.* Amityville, NY. Vajra Press, 1993.

American Psychological Association. (2013). *Stress in America: Missing the Health Care Connection.* Retrieved from http://www.apa.org/news/press/releases/stress/2012/full-report.pdf

American Psychological Association. (2013a). *Communication Technology: Implications for Work and Well-Being.* Retrieved from http://www.apaexcellence.org/assets/general/2013-work-and-communication- technology-survey-final.pdf

American Psychological Association. (2013b). *2013 Work and Well-Being Survey.* Retrieved from http://www.apaexcellence.org/assets/general/2013-work-and-wellbeing- survey-results.pdf

American Psychological Association. (2012). *Workforce Retention Survey.* Retrieved from http://www.apaexcellence.org/assets/general/2012-retention-survey-final.pdf

American Psychological Association. (2009). *Stress in America 2009.* Retrieved from http://www.apa.org/news/press/releases/stress-exec-summary.pdf

American Psychological Association (2004). *Employer Recommendations. Public Policy, Work, and Families: The Report of the APA Presidential Initiative on Work and Families.* Retrieved from http://www.apa.org/work-family/employers.html

Blessing, B. & Gibbins, I. "Autonomic Nervous System, Fig.1"

Scholarpedia 3(7) (2008): 2787.

Mann, Denise (2013) (reviewed by Laura J. Martin, M.D.). Alcohol and a Good Night's Sleep Don't Mix. Retrieved from http://www.webmd.com/sleep-disorders/news/20130118/alcohol-sleep

Bureau of Labor Statistics. (2001). [Table R67] *Number and percent distribution of nonfatal occupational injuries and illnesses involving days away from work by nature of injury or illness and number of days away from work.* Retrieved from http://www.bls.gov/iif/oshwc/osh/case/ostb1222.pdf

Cannon, W.B. (1929). *Bodily Changes in Pain, Hunger, Fear, and Rage.* New York and London. D. Appelton and Company, 1915.

Frone, M. R., Russell, M., & Barnes, G. M. Work-Family Conflict, Gender and Health Related Outcomes: A study of employed parents in two community samples. *Journal of Occupational Health Psychology, 1,* (1996): 57-69.

Holmes, T. H. & Rahe R. H. The Social Readjustment Rating Scale. *Journal of Psychosomatic Research,* Volume 11, Issue 2, (1967).

Kabat-Zinn, Jon. *Wherever You Go, There You Are: Mindfulness meditation in every-day life.* New York, NY. Hyperion, 1994.

Kabat-Zinn, Jon. *Full Catastrophe Living: Using the wisdom of your body and mind to face stress, pain, and illness.* McHenry, IL. Delta Publishing Company, 1990.

Lehrer, P., Woolfolk, R. L. & Sime W. E. *Principles and Practice of Stress Management,* New York, NY. Guilford Press, 1993.

Davis, M., Eshelman, E. R., & McKay, M. *The Relaxation and Stress Reduction Workbook,* 6th Ed. Oakland, CA. New Harbinger Publications, 2008.

Neal, M. N. & Hammer, L. B. *Working Couples Caring for Children and Aging Parents: Effects on work-family fit, well-being, and work (a longitudinal study funded by the Alfred P. Sloan Foundation).* Mahwah, NJ. Lawrence Erlbaum Associates, 2007.

Priest, Simon. *The Adventure Experience Paradigm.* In J.C. Miles, & S. Priest (Eds.), Adventure Recreation. State College PA: Venture Publishing, 1990.

PubMed Health: Informed Health Online. Institute for Quality and Efficiency in Health Care (IQWiG) What Is Burnout Syndrome? Retrieved from http://www.ncbi.nlm.nih.gov/pubmedhealth/PMH0050545/

Rosch, P. J. *The Quandary of Job Stress Compensation.* Health and Stress, Volume 3, 1-4 (2001).

Sagawa Y., Kondo H., Matsubuchi N., et. al. Alcohol Has a Dose-Related Effect on Parasympathetic Nerve Activity During Sleep, Alcoholism: *Clinical and Experimental Research,* Volume 35, Issue 11 (2011).

Shaar, M. & Britton, K. *Smarts and Stamina: The busy person's guide to optimal health and performance.* New York, NY. Positive Psychology Press, 2011.

Tan, Chade-Meng. *Search Inside Yourself: The Unexpected Path to Achieving Success, Happiness (and World Peace).* New York, NY. Harper Collins, 2012.

Tartakovsky, Margarita. (2011). Is Technology Running Your Life? Set Some

Boundaries. Retrieved from *PsychCentral*.com http://psychcentral.com/lib/
is-technology-running-your-life-set-some-boundaries/0008730

Tartakovsky, Margarita. (2011). 10 Ways to Build and Preserve Better
Boundaries. *Psych Central*. Retrieved on October 23, 2014, from http://psy-
chcentral.com/lib/10-way-to-build-and-preserve-better-boundaries/0007498

Yerkes R. M. & Dodson J. D. *The Relation of Strength of Stimulus to Rapidity of Habit-Formation.* Journal of Comparative Neurology and Psychology
Volume 18, 459–482 (1908).

STRESS AND SELF-CARE IN THE WORKPLACE

Throughout this book, we discussed stress management and self-care as it applies to the individual in personal and family life. In a follow up book to *From Stressed to Centered: A Practical Guide to a Healthier and Happier You*, we will discuss the unique stressors that typically occur within the workplace and how to address those to maximize organizational performance and employee well-being.

Key Contributors to Workplace Stress

In our current work as executive coaches/consultants, we have identified several key contributors to workplace stress, which include:

High demand to multi-task

Unrealistic expectations by managers and employees

Employee overload (understaffing)

Role ambiguity (expectations within the organization)

Unmanageable/unresolved conflict in relationships at work

Unconstructive, untimely, or disingenuous feedback

Difficulties with delegation

Incongruous organization-employee values

Organizational boundary ambiguity (i.e., open door policy, accessibility while on vacation, under-responsiveness to abuse in the workplace)

Impact of Workplace Stress on Employees and Organizations

Statistics show that the American workforce is under stress:

> Sixty-nine percent of employees report that work is a significant source of stress, and 41 percent say they typically feel tense or stressed out during the workday (American Psychological Association, 2009).

So what? Well, let's look at the next statistic:

> Unmanaged stress and stress-related issues cost US companies, nationally, over 300 billion dollars a year on average in absenteeism, turnover, diminished productivity, and medical, legal, and insurance costs (Rosch, 2001).

> Fifty-one percent of employees said they were less productive at work as a result of stress (American Psychological Association, 2009).

Can Your Company Really Afford to Ignore This?

The purpose of our next book is to provide upper-level managers, executives, leaders, human resource professionals, and OD leaders with an evidence-based framework addressing the relationship between stress management and self-care in the workplace and positive organizational outcomes. We will discuss how to effectively identify and assess workplace stressors and self-care deficits within your organization. We will present the best practices to effectively address these problems and create a culture of health and resilience to stress. Finally, we will offer examples of successful applications of these best practices by US organizations as an effective starting point.